A Stream of Light

Unitarian Universalist Association, 25 Beacon Street, Boston, Massachusetts

A Stream of Light

A Short History of American Unitarianism

Edited by Conrad Wright

Boston: Skinner House Books

Preface

The first edition of this book marked the 150th anniversary of the American Unitarian Association. The preface to that 1975 edition warned that the book did not constitute a definitive treatment of the subject, for two reasons in particular.

In the first place, a "revolution" in American Unitarian historiography was in progress, as scholars of a new generation engaged in rewriting the story of pre-Civil War Unitarianism. They had new emphases and somewhat altered judgments with respect to familiar figures in the history of the denomination. After a century or more in which Unitarian history was written almost entirely with a pro-Transcendentalist bias, the conservative Unitarians against whom the Transcendentalists rebelled were being examined with some degree of sympathy.

In the second place, a problem existed because little attention had been given by scholars to the period since 1865. That field was described as little-known territory.

The historiographical revolution has continued. But it has not sought sympathy for the conservative Unitarians as much as suggested that earlier scholarship overstated the sharp contrast between the "Unitarians" and the "Transcendentalists." If Andrews Norton is taken as the type figure of the older generation and Ralph Waldo Emerson as the type figure of the younger one, Emerson's *Divinity School Address* (1838) and Norton's *Latest Form of Infidelity* (1839) suggest a dramatic confrontation. But many who agreed with

viii   *A Stream of Light*

Norton's theology and respected his scholarship were severely critical of his rhetoric and manner, and denied that he spoke for them.
There were also Transcendentalists—Frederic H. Hedge, James F.
Clarke, and even Theodore Parker, are examples—who were critical
of some of the tendencies of Emerson's thought, even as they
acknowledged his power and maintained warm friendship with him.
Between Norton at one extreme and Emerson at the other was a
spectrum, not a gulf. Emerson left the ministry, but most of the
Transcendentalists served Unitarian churches throughout their
careers. They could do so because their "transcendentalism" was as
much a development within the Unitarian tradition as a response to
new currents of thought. Historical scholarship has become increasingly aware of the continuities between Transcendentalism and the
older Unitarianism that nurtured it.

The scholarship of the last decade-and-a-half has continued to emphasize the pre-Civil War period; the latter part of that century still
needs much careful study. We do have recent biographies of Henry
W. Bellows and Samuel A. Eliot, and Francis Greenwood Peabody
has attracted the attention of more than one scholar. But those who
enjoy exploring little-known territory will find here rich materials
easily accessible.

More good work of Unitarian historical scholarship is being
produced today than was the case a generation ago, and even the
more neglected field of Universalist scholarship shows signs of life.
The Unitarian Universalist Historical Society is more active and its
Proceedings has achieved wider recognition. The Unitarian Universalist Association, in collaboration with the Massachusetts Historical
Society, has underwritten fellowships for research in Unitarian and
Universalist history. The denomination is still not in danger of being
tyrannized by tradition or of becoming a prisoner of the past; but
there seems to be—at the moment, at least—more awareness of the
extent to which the collective memory of a people can reinforce its
present endeavors and make more effective its response to the
challenges that confront it.

Conrad Wright
Cambridge, Massachusetts, 1989

Contents

Introduction

The American Unitarian Association was organized on May 25, 1825. But first there had to be Channing's Baltimore Sermon in 1819; and before that, the dispute over the election of Henry Ware as Hollis Professor of Divinity in 1805, an event which has long been taken to have been the starting point of the Unitarian Controversy.

Yet we cannot understand the history of American Unitarianism in the nineteenth century without looking back to the eighteenth, and even farther back than that. Unitarianism was not a sudden new creation in 1805. It was a product of the impact on New England Puritanism of the eighteenth-century currents of thought that we refer to, in shorthand expression, as the Enlightenment, or the Age of Reason.[1] Before examining Unitarianism as a distinct religious movement, or denomination, we must remind ourselves of some of the continuities between it and the Puritanism from which it emerged.

There were, first of all, doctrinal continuities. To be sure, it is easy to emphasize the points of discontinuity, where the liberals rejected the position of their orthodox parents or grandparents. The Puritans saw God first and foremost as sovereign and judge, and emphasized his righteous will in the condemnation of sinners; the liberals preferred to think of him as a loving father, with a benevolent concern for the salvation of all mankind. The Puritans saw unregenerate human nature as depraved, and corrupted by

xi

Adam's sin; the liberals saw it as having the capacity for righteousness as well as for sin, and insisted that what human beings do in
this life will have a real bearing on their salvation. The Puritans
believed that Scripture reveals a triune God; the liberals argued
that the doctrine of the Trinity is both unscriptural and irrational.
But the frame of reference within which all these issues were
disputed was the reformed theology of the Westminster Confession. The liberals gave unorthodox answers, but the questions
were not unorthodox questions. If the liberals were unorthodox
in their responses, they were nevertheless quite orthodox in accepting those questions as the important ones that had to be
addressed. This means that one of the most important factors in
the shaping of Unitarianism was the theology of John Calvin. As
between Calvin and Servetus, or Calvin and the Socini, who has
had the greatest influence on American Unitarianism? Which one
is the ancestor? Calvin, of course.

There were also continuities in terms of ecclesiastical structure.
It has been argued, not entirely facetiously, that the only things
on which Unitarian Universalists agree are congregational polity
and Robert's rules of order. Congregational polity, at any rate, is
not a Unitarian invention, nor do Unitarian Universalists have a
monopoly of it. As they proclaim its virtues, or appeal to it as
normative for their way of ordering their affairs, they should
remember that it is theirs by inheritance from William Ames, and
John Cotton, and Thomas Hooker. The Unitarian Universalist
Association is the kind of organization it is, at least in part, because the Cambridge Platform of Church Discipline was recommended to the churches of New England in 1648.

There were, and are, continuities also in terms of accepted
values. Puritanism eludes simple definition; but one may at least
say that one mark of the Puritan was his conviction that serious
matters should be taken seriously, religion first and foremost
among them. His religion involved both his duty to his Creator,
and his obligations to his fellow human beings; and it imposed
on him the responsibility for constant self-scrutiny to be sure that
he was doing what he ought, and as much as he ought. This
quality of "moral athleticism" [2] long outlasted the doctrinal
formulations with which it was originally associated.

In the course of the eighteenth century, the New England Puritan tradition broke into two streams, one of them "evangelical," the other "rationalistic." The crucial event was the Great Awakening of 1740-43, when Jonathan Edwards, George Whitefield, Gilbert Tennent, and other revivalists sought to recapture a sense of the immediacy of the Holy Spirit in the conversion of souls. They succeeded in revitalizing Calvinistic theology and in establishing a revivalistic tradition, but it was too late to re-establish an undivided religious community on that basis. There were those, like Charles Chauncy (1705-1787), who were dismayed by the emotional excesses of the Great Awakening and declared it a corruption of religion. "There is the Religion of the *Understanding* and *Judgment*, and *Will*, as well as of the *Affections*," he wrote; "and if little Account is made of the *former*, while great Stress is laid upon the *latter*, it can't be but People should run into Disorders." [3] Here, in the clash between the supporters and the opposers of the Great Awakening, may be discerned the line of cleavage that was to be ever more deeply scored until the communion of the churches of the Standing Order in New England was finally shattered in the Unitarian Controversy.

For the revivalists, the experience of conversion was congruent with the Calvinistic doctrines of original sin and predestination. For the opposers, a rejection of the necessity for the experience ultimately led to a rejection of the structure of doctrine within which it made sense. That is to say, by abandoning the notion of conversion as a sudden tumultuous event, and replacing it with a concept of conversion as a gradual process, the opposers were led to a definition of human nature in which the capacity to respond to God's gracious promises was ascribed to all humans. This assertion of human ability was called Arminianism, as when Jonathan Edwards declared, speaking of the year 1734: "About this time began the great noise that was in this part of the country, about Arminianism, which seemed to appear with a very threatening aspect upon the interest of religion here." Arminianism developed rapidly in New England in the middle decades of the eighteenth century, especially in eastern Massachusetts in the churches of the Standing Order, and in Connecticut in the Church of England.

Arminianism stood for heightened confidence in the capacity of human beings to *do* the will of God. Rationalism, as the term was applied to religion, meant an enhanced confidence in human capacity, by the use of reason, to *know* the will of God.[4] The rise of modern science stimulated its growth, and Newton and Locke formulated its philosophical presuppositions. Two kinds of religious rationalism were the result. The more uncompromising kind, termed Deism, rejected Christianity, and asserted the sufficiency of Natural Religion—that is to say, those religious truths that may be discovered by the unassisted reason: the existence of God, our obligations of piety towards the Creator and benevolence towards our fellow men, and a future state of rewards and punishments. The less radical kind of religious rationalism, sometimes called Supernatural Rationalism, acknowledged the validity of Natural Religion but denied its sufficiency. Natural Religion, it was argued, must be supplemented with Revealed Religion; and Christianity is such a religion, whose supernatural origin and divine sanction are attested by the fact that Christ fulfilled prophecy and performed miracles. These claims of Christianity to be a revealed religion are themselves subject to rational test, in accordance with the same canons of evidence that one applies to any historical event. It was this Supernatural Rationalism, and not Deism, that the New England liberals accepted; and it was their commitment to it that explains the reaction of conservative Unitarians to Transcendentalism in the 1830s.

In the closing years of the eighteenth century, the New England liberals began to question the doctrine of the Trinity, primarily on the grounds that it is unscriptural. Hence, by the time of the outbreak of the Unitarian Controversy, the Liberal Christians—as they then preferred to call themselves—had rounded out a structure of doctrine that was Arminian as to the doctrines of grace, rationalistic as to epistemology, and antitrinitarian as to Christology. This combination of ideas, constructed over the course of two generations by such men as Charles Chauncy and Jonathan Mayhew, represented the intellectual capital on which the liberals drew in the years of controversy after 1805.

A Stream of Light

Chapter 1

"Elected Now by Time"

The Unitarian Controversy, 1805-1835

I

The election of Henry Ware in 1805 as Hollis Professor of Divinity at Harvard precipitated the Unitarian Controversy that was to divide the congregational churches of the Standing Order in New England. Yet already by that date, liberal thought under the guise of Arminianism had flourished for half a century within Massachusetts Congregationalism. Charles Chauncy (1705-1787) and Jonathan Mayhew (1720-1766) had led the way in contesting Calvinistic doctrines of original sin and eternal punishment. By the time of the American Revolution, it was not uncommon to find clergymen who had ceased to make any reference in their sermons to the doctrine of the Trinity. They held Arian views of the nature of Christ, by which the Son was declared to be subordinate to the Father.

Illustrative of men of this spirit in the closing decades of the century was Dr. Prince of the First Church in Salem, whose remarkable library was well stocked with books of the most advanced thought of the day, among them those of the foremost English Unitarians. Typical, too, was his near neighbor, Dr. Thomas Barnard of Salem's North Church. Barnard had no taste for doctrinal debate, and consequently refrained from discussing disputed points of theology. One of his parishioners, aware of his reluctance, once said to him: "Dr. Barnard, I never heard you

3

preach a sermon upon the Trinity." His reply was to the point: "And you never will." [1]

These men represent religious liberalism developing within the churches of the Standing Order. Similar tendencies within the Church of England also produced an important defection from orthodox views of the Trinity, when James Freeman led King's Chapel in Boston to an explicit acknowledgment of the Unitarian position. Born in 1759, Freeman graduated from Harvard College in the class of 1777. He was invited to serve as lay reader at King's Chapel in 1782. On December 24 of that year, he wrote his father:

> I suppose, long before this reaches you, you will be made acquainted with my situation at the Chapel. I am now confirmed in the opinion that I shall obtain the settlement for life. The church increases every day, and I am happy to find that my friends are still very partial. . . . I have fortunately no temptations to be bigoted, for the proprietors of the Chapel are very liberal in their notions. They allow me to make several alterations in the service, which liberty I frequently use. We can scarcely be called of the Church of England, for we disclaim the authority of that country in ecclesiastical as well as in civil matters.[2]

In the following two years, his views on the Trinity so changed that he expected that he would be obliged to resign his post. But after he stated his position on the subject in a series of sermons, the congregation voted, on June 19, 1785, to amend the liturgy of the Prayer Book, bringing it into conformity with Freeman's views. Thus, in the words of his successor, F. W. P. Greenwood, "the first Episcopal Church in New England became the first Unitarian Church in the New World."

In 1783, Freeman made application to Bishop Seabury of Connecticut and Bishop Provoost of New York, requesting ordination. He confided in a letter to his father that the request would in all likelihood be denied. The following spring, the Committee of King's Chapel took the occasion of a visit to Boston by Bishop Seabury to talk with him further, pressing for the ordination of Freeman and asking that he be required only to give assent to his faith in the Holy Scriptures. Still a decision was delayed, and three months later, Freeman was before the Episcopal Convention in Stratford, Connecticut, responding to questions regarding the changes he had introduced in the Prayer Book. They consisted of the deletion of references to the Trinity and the revision of

King's Chapel

prayers addressed to the Son and to the Holy Spirit. When asked what scriptural support he found for his rejection of the Trinity, he cited two passages: "There is one God, and one Mediator between God and Man, the man Christ Jesus" (I Timothy 2:5); "There is but one God, the Father, and one Lord Jesus Christ" (I Corinthians 8:6). Delay followed until, growing increasingly restive, the congregation itself ordained Freeman at Evening Prayer on November 18, 1787.

Freeman was more directly influenced by English Unitarianism than were the liberals in the congregational churches, and his antitrinitarianism was more radical than theirs. For them, Christ was created before the beginning of the world, though not part of the Godhead. Freeman's Christology, unlike theirs, was Socinian rather than Arian; that is to say, he believed that Christ was a man, rather than a superangelic being, though chosen of God to be in a unique way the channel of divine revelation. Outside New England, English Socinianism was represented by Joseph Priestley, who migrated to the New World and settled in Pennsylvania in 1794. Although Freeman was the only declared Unitarian minister in Boston, he was not wanting in liberal associates. John Eliot of the New North Church, John T. Kirkland of the New South, and his classmate, William Bentley of Salem, were close friends. In the first years of his ministry, he was excluded from the circle of Episcopal clergy and as yet was not counted among the Congregational clergy; but he came to be universally respected by his colleagues on both sides. He was a staunch friend to a good number of the younger men who a generation later would themselves bear the Unitarian label.

By the end of the eighteenth century, the number of voices raised in opposition to one or another aspect of Calvinistic theology was clearly on the increase. The points most disputed were the notion of original sin, election, the place of individual responsibility, and the traditional view of the atonement. More than a few earnest Christians were concerned that the Calvinistic system of salvation was on the one hand far too complex, while on the other it placed too little emphasis on the importance of personal responsibility for the conduct of a moral life. There was indeed a widely felt need for a simplification of the Christian message that would give greater attention to the ethical concerns of religion.

The reasons for the growing criticism of the theology that had reigned in New England for close to two centuries were several. Political philosophies that had nurtured the growth of democracy stressed individual initiative and responsibility. Dogmatic assertions of the bondage of the will in the religious sphere were manifestly absurd. Rationalism, one of the two major movements in eighteenth-century thought, was slowly but inevitably making its impact on the New England theology. In addition to these factors, there should be mentioned the Arminianism of two generations and the lingering effects of the Great Awakening, each in its own way destined to give an impetus to change within the Standing Order. Within Massachusetts Congregationalism, a considerable range of views might be discerned, from the New Divinity of the followers of Edwards at one extreme, to liberalism at the other. Finally, while Congregationalism was still dominant in New England, the rapid growth of Protestant pluralism was well under way. In 1800, there appear to have been 344 Congregational churches in Massachusetts. The remaining 151 churches included 93 Baptist, 29 Methodist, 14 Episcopal, 8 Friends Meetings, 4 Universalist, 2 Presbyterian, and one Roman Catholic, the first building for which was constructed that year.[3]

As the century turned, the ecclesiastical fabric remained generally intact. Here and there divisions had occurred. In 1785, Aaron Bancroft candidated in Worcester, but his liberalism was unacceptable to the majority of the church. A Second Parish was organized by his supporters. No articles of belief were adopted, but the guiding principle that characterized the liberalism of the time was proclaimed, namely adherence to the Bible as containing "the sufficient rule of faith and practice." The parish in Taunton, similarly, divided in 1792.

In Plymouth, the ancient Church and Parish of Pilgrim founding had been disturbed by the revivalistic sympathies of its minister, Chandler Robbins, and by the Calvinistic confession of faith introduced in 1795 replacing the broader covenant that had been in force since 1676. The liberals were patient until Dr. Robbins's death in 1799 ended a ministry of 41 years, when they found themselves to be in the majority, and so settled a liberal, James Kendall. The orthodox thereupon withdrew and formed a separate church.

But these were exceptional instances. For two decades more, the hope was cherished that in spite of the growing religious diversity the unity of the congregational Standing Order might be preserved.

II

The Hollis Professorship of Divinity was the oldest endowed chair in America, established in Harvard College in 1721 by the will of Thomas Hollis, a London merchant. The third incumbent, Dr. David Tappan, known as a moderate Calvinist, died in 1803. The election of a successor turned out to be of such moment, and the ensuing debate so bitter, that Harvard's historian, Samuel Eliot Morison, has described the controversy as "a college revolution." When the outcome was finally known, the liberals were found to be in control of the college that had been a veritable cornerstone of Calvinism and the New England Standing Order.[4]

When Dr. Tappan died, there was clearly no stronger candidate for the Hollis chair than the distinguished minister of Hingham's First Parish, the Reverend Henry Ware. But Ware was known to be a liberal. Indeed, he and his colleague, Dr. Daniel Shute of Hingham's Second Parish, had collaborated in preparing for use in their parishes a catechism which was clearly Arian in its Christology. President Joseph Willard of Harvard, himself a moderate Calvinist, was thought to be hopeful that another moderate might be chosen. But when President Willard died suddenly in 1804, the Corporation—one of Harvard's two governing bodies—was faced with the task of filling not one, but two positions of critical importance.

The Corporation decided to fill the professorship and then to turn to the matter of choosing a president. The six members of the Corporation were: Ebenezer Storer, a Boston merchant and the college treasurer; Eliphalet Pearson, Hancock Professor and acting president; Judge John Davis of Plymouth and Boston; Oliver Wendell of Boston; and the ministers of two of the Boston churches, the Second and the New North, Dr. John Lathrop and

John Eliot respectively. Theologically, Wendell and Pearson might be counted orthodox, while the four other members held liberal sentiments. Yet when the voting began, it was demonstrably not along party lines, for a stalemate resulted.

At a meeting in December, 1804, after considerable discussion, each member offered two names in nomination for the professorship. Pearson and Wendell put forth the names of two conservatives, the Reverend Jesse Appleton of Hampton, New Hampshire, and the Reverend Joshua Bates of Dedham. Davis and Eliot proposed the names of two liberals: the Reverend Henry Ware and the Reverend John Pierce of Brookline. The two remaining members of the Corporation each offered the name of a liberal and a conservative: Lathrop proposed Ware and Bates, while Storer offered the names of Ware and a "Mr. Payson," presumably the Reverend Seth Payson of Rindge, New Hampshire. In the ensuing discussion, it appeared that the members of the Corporation were equally divided between Ware and Appleton. A compromise was proposed, by which Ware would become President, while Appleton would be named Professor. Ware received four votes for President, but Appleton got only three for Hollis Professor, so the compromise failed. The Corporation finally, on February 1, 1805, gave the professorship to Ware by a vote of four to two.

Now the Overseers had to confirm. That the issue was regarded as one of serious import is clear from the large attendance at the meeting. Of the Board of Overseers, 57 of the 64 members were present: 45 of the 47 lay members and 12 of the 17 clerical members. The debate was intense. The terms of the Hollis bequest were discussed and weighed: that the officers of the college should "prefer a man of solid learning in divinity, of sound and orthodox principles." To the orthodox, led by the unyielding Dr. Jedidiah Morse of Charlestown, this could mean but one thing: the incumbent must be a Calvinist, fully prepared to subscribe to the Westminster Confession. To the liberals, however, this surely was not the intent. After all, Thomas Hollis was, himself, a Baptist, whose own minister had refused to make the Westminster Confession a test of orthodoxy, claiming the Bible as his only authority. And although the terms of the bequest had been drawn up by others, Hollis had personally added to their stipulations one of his own, namely, that the only article of belief to be required of the professor should be that "the Bible is the only and most perfect rule of faith and practice," which should be interpreted "according to the best light that God should give him." The minutes of the meeting of the Overseers state only the outcome; but according to Jedidiah Morse, the vote was 33 to 23 in favor of Ware.

The liberals had won the day, and Harvard had, in their eyes, shown that its allegiance was "to Christ and not to Calvin." [5] To the orthodox, the matter appeared in a quite different light. A few weeks after the fateful meeting, Morse published a pamphlet entitled: *The True Reasons on Which the Election of a Hollis Professor of Divinity in Harvard College Was Opposed at the Board of Overseers, Feb. 14, 1805.* In it he called attention to the motto of the college—*Christo et Ecclesiae*—and wrote:

"For CHRIST and the CHURCH," was this ancient college founded by men, whom we delight to call our Fathers; "for CHRIST and the CHURCH" has it hitherto been cherished, instructed and governed by men of like Christian principles and spirit. . . . Oh may the GOD of our Fathers, who still lives and reigns, in mercy preserve it, so long as the sun and moon shall endure![6]

A year later, Samuel Webber, another liberal, became president of the college, and before the end of the decade, liberal control was no more contested. Indeed, in 1807 the orthodox, deeming Harvard unfit to prepare men of their persuasion for the ministry, had founded Andover Seminary. Nine years after Andover's founding, the orthodox established another seminary in Bangor, Maine. Yale soon followed with its divinity school in 1822, and when its liberalism became apparent, another came into existence at East Windsor Hill, later to become the Hartford Theological Seminary.[7]

Did the series of events at Harvard signal a liberal victory or sectarian defeat? For upwards of half a century, Calvinists and Arminians had worked together in harmony. Liberals earnestly hoped that the unity of Congregationalism could be preserved. But partisan rivalries did not subside. The Unitarian Controversy was under way!

III

Jedidiah Morse led the orthodox reaction to Ware's election. Born in 1761, he had graduated from Yale College in 1783, and six years later he became the minister of the First Church in Charlestown, Massachusetts. From the time of his arrival in Boston, he sensed a pervasive liberal sentiment he could not share. The Congregationalism of his native Connecticut breathed different air. In Boston the spirit of Harvard, long the stronghold of moderate Calvinism, had impressed itself on the life of the churches. In 1790, one year after his arrival, he took the occasion at three of the Great and Thursday Lectures to speak on the divinity of Christ. Already he saw himself cast in the role of defender of Christian orthodoxy. Even before the controversy over Ware's appointment as Hollis Professor, Morse's strategy was taking shape. His biographer stated it thus:

> It cannot be doubted that Dr. Morse early formed the purpose of doing his utmost to effect an important change in the ecclesiastical condition of Massachusetts—first, by separating the Unitarians from the Orthodox, and then, by drawing the Orthodox of different shades into more intimate relations.[8]

It was an effective plan that Morse set in motion. After 1805, the liberal party could be more clearly defined by its approval of the choice of Ware, and its continued confidence in Harvard College and its governing authorities. The Old Calvinists and the Hopkinsians (or New Divinity men) combined in support of the Andover Theological Seminary. The grand design of separation became apparent in 1812, when the newly settled minister of the Second Church in Dorchester, John Codman, declared that he would not exchange pulpits with liberal clergymen. This was the first step in destroying the unity of the ecclesiastical order, since one of the long established and jealously guarded symbols of fellowship among the New England churches was the custom of the monthly pulpit exchange. Codman and the orthodox party would have been hard put to find a more effective way of signalling the changed temper of the times. The spirit of exclusion was rending the robe of Christ's church. It was the first victory of sectarianism, lamented by all persons of irenic temper then and since.

IV

Unitarianism began as a biblical religion. While Unitarians acknowledged that certain basic religious truths, such as the existence of God, may be established by the use of the reason, God's plan for the salvation of human souls is made known to us through revelation, of which the record is found in the pages of the Bible. Hence the science of biblical criticism was regarded by the liberal Christians as central in the theological training of the minister.[9]

During the eighteenth century, Americans were familiar with the methods of biblical criticism and exegesis available to them in British works, but German critical scholarship was virtually unknown to them. It was just as the Unitarian Controversy was developing that American liberals became aware of the work done by such scholars as Michaelis and Griesbach. They seized on it eagerly, since its finds promised to support them in their debate with the orthodox. After all, the chief argument against the doctrine of the Trinity was that it was unscriptural. A correct understanding of the Bible, they were confident, would assure the triumph of liberal Christianity.

In the introduction of German biblical criticism to these shores, Joseph Stevens Buckminster played a crucial role. His career was cut short by his untimely death at the age of 28; but despite his youth, his impact on his contemporaries was so great that scholars are sometimes tempted to refer to the "Age of Buckminster." Even half a century after his death, his influence was still felt. John Gorham Palfrey assessed his importance in these terms:

> An admiring company of young men was inspired with his generous love of learning. Norton, Ticknor, Frothingham, the Everetts, were among those who came within the circle of his personal companionship. Sparks, Prescott, Bancroft, felt the influence at a further remove. The more numerous scholars who have won a name in later days, have known him only by the traditions of their circle; but the propitious atmosphere in which their genius has been unfolded owes more of its nourishing quality to no other mind.[10]

Buckminster was born in Portsmouth, New Hampshire, in 1784. His father, the Reverend Dr. Joseph Buckminster, was a staunch defender of the orthodoxy of the times. The young Buckminster's keen mind early showed itself in his prodigious reading and in his accomplishments in the study of languages. He began the study of Latin at the age of four, and a year later commenced the study of Greek. By the time of his graduation from Harvard College at the age of 16 he had made his mark in Classics and had added Hebrew and French to the languages at his command. At Exeter Academy, where he was a tutor in the Classics until 1802, he read widely in Greek literature and in the field of Patristics while preparing himself for the ministry. For another two years, he lived as a tutor in Waltham, Massachusetts, with sufficient leisure to broaden his range of study, which now included an ever deepening investigation into the thought of English Unitarians and Deists. Now, too, he discovered the more advanced work in biblical criticism being carried on in Europe, and especially in Germany, but which had made little headway in England and had not at all been felt in America.

Living in Waltham, Buckminster was able to renew his associations with Boston and Cambridge friends, and especially with Dr. Freeman, a relative by marriage, whose influence on his thinking, now rapidly taking shape, was considerable. Young Buckminster often attended services at King's Chapel, and, in spite of his respect for his father's opinions, finally acknowledged that his studies had led him to an acceptance of Arian views. For a time he delayed his plans for entering the ministry, even refusing an invitation to become Dr. Freeman's assistant. In 1804, however, he was examined for the ministry by the Boston Association and called soon after to the pulpit of one of the most distinguished congregations in the city, the Brattle Street Church. He was already settled as its minister when he marked his twenty-first birthday.

Buckminster early and justifiably earned the reputation of being in the intellectual forefront of the Boston clergy. He had no peer in his study and grasp of the principles and implications of biblical criticism. He saw the importance of the distinction made between Gospels and Epistles by John Locke a century earlier. For the first time, the traditional unity of the Bible was being challenged. To discover the real meaning of Scripture, one must deal with questions of authorship, date, purpose, and the character of each of its parts. Buckminster soon became acquainted with the pioneering work of Bishop Lowth on Hebrew poetry, *De Sacra Poesi Hebraeorum* (1753), which had resulted in a further work of far-reaching importance by the same scholar, namely, his commentary on Isaiah (1778).

In Germany the new era of biblical study was marked by the work of J. G. Eichhorn and J. G. von Herder. But the single greatest discovery for Buckminster in these exciting years was J. D. Michaelis's New Testament *Introduction*, just recently translated from the German. The most radical views of the age regarding the canonical status of the several New Testament books were advanced by Michaelis. The whole question of inspiration and authority was being explored for the first time by the young minister of the Brattle Street Church, who was now fully in touch with the ferment of ideas that would soon play a critical role in the theological controversies disturbing the New England churches.

In failing health, Buckminster was sent off by his congregation in 1806 for a year of travel in Europe. His health was not restored, but he seized the moment to gather a scholar's library. By his journey's end, he possessed some 3,000 volumes, including Griesbach's critical edition of the Greek New Testament. This was to be the basic tool for Buckminster's subsequent work in criticism. His library was said to comprise the rarest collection of scholarly books of any privately held collection in New England.

In 1807, he persuaded Harvard College to undertake an American printing of Griesbach's New Testament, Buckminster himself correcting the proofs and seeing the work through the press. Between 1805 and 1812, the *Monthly Anthology* published eight of Buckminster's papers; these, together with two volumes of his sermons published posthumously, reveal him to have been not only Boston's most eloquent preacher but without a rival as a responsible and able practitioner of the new criticism.[11]

What were the ideas that Buckminster advanced, thereby bringing into sharp relief the differences between the orthodox and the liberal parties? He maintained complete confidence in the principle that the Bible is the final authority in all matters of Christian theology. Here the two parties were at one. But, he argued, scholarly study of the Bible is essential to discover the true meaning of Scripture. Such study discloses that the positions dearly held by the orthodox, who presume them to be derived from the Bible, are in reality based on creeds and dogmatic systems. These systems do not proceed from Scripture, but, rather, are imposed upon it. It is "from our having taken our religious opinions from authority, and not from the scriptures," he declared, "that we see so much uncertainty and contradiction among Protestants." [12]

The two critical principles Buckminster used were, first, a scrupulously careful study of the New Testament text; and second, the application of historical methodology to the investigation of the complex questions of the canon and inspiration of the Bible.[13] The application of these principles to the study of the New Testament—Buckminster was not especially interested in the Old Testament—led the young scholar and preacher to the conclusion that the question of inspiration was crucial for understanding differences between orthodox and liberal Christians. The orthodox regarded the Bible as uniformly inspired, and therefore were obliged to reconcile all parts of Scripture. Buckminster had been persuaded by the views of Michaelis that the New Testament books were canonized not because they were inspired but because they were written by inspired men, by the Apostles. The Scriptures were the products of men of first-century Palestine, themselves subject to the influences of their own time and place, sharing the world-view of their age. The Bible communicates truth and so it *contains* authoritative statements, yet not all Scripture is equally authoritative! In short, the Bible is not God's word, but is the *vehicle* by which that word comes to us.

Since not all parts of the New Testament could lay claim to apostolic authorship, one must distinguish between the "Received Canon" and the "True Canon." For Buckminster, the heart of the Christian revelation is to be found in the Gospels. The historical facts of Jesus' life and message, confirmed by authenticated prophecy and the presence of miraculous events, establish the bedrock of the Christian proclamation: Jesus is the Messiah.

In setting forth the grounds for the unqualified acceptance of the Gospels, Buckminster was careful to make a place for the use of reason. Those who built on the foundation laid by him, and especially Channing in his efforts to recover a pure and reasonable

Christianity, were to articulate the legitimacy of reason as another means for authenticating revelation.

In 1810, the bequest of Samuel Dexter provided for the establishment of a lectureship on Biblical criticism at Harvard, thereby opening the way for the first instruction in the new criticism to be offered anywhere in America. Buckminster was the obvious choice to fill the new post as Dexter Lecturer, and the appointment was made in 1811. He began at once to plan his first series of lectures, at the same time preparing to embark on the study of German in order to keep himself thoroughly abreast of the rapid developments in the new science of criticism. Tragically, death interrupted his preparations three months before he was to assume his new duties. The end came in 1812, a few weeks after his twenty-eighth birthday. He had set the course for making use of the tools of criticism in exploring questions of Christian origins and the nature of authority. These were the issues that would determine the shape of the debate between the liberal and orthodox parties for another generation.

V

The task that Jedidiah Morse had set for himself of separating liberal Christians from their orthodox brethren was taken up in earnest when there fell into his hands a copy of Thomas Belsham's biography of Theophilus Lindsey. Published in London in 1812, it contained extracts from the correspondence between Lindsey and several liberal ministers in the Boston area, beginning in 1786 and continuing for several years. Here there was an account of the progress of Unitarian opinion in New England. Morse excerpted the chapter from Belsham's *Life*, reprinting it as a pamphlet under a title of his own devising: *American Unitarianism*. In his Preface, he not only implied that the New England liberals shared the more radical views of the English Unitarians, like Belsham, but directly accused them of concealing "from the mass of the Christian community their ultimate designs." [14]

American Unitarianism was promptly reviewed by Jeremiah Evarts, a close associate of Morse, in the *Panoplist*, of which Morse himself was the editor. Evarts's attack on the liberals made three basic points: (1) English Unitarianism and the views of the New

England liberal Christians may safely be assumed to be identical; (2) the liberals were less than honest in cloaking their true views in secrecy while advancing them, thereby putting in jeopardy the true faith espoused by the orthodox; (3) liberals ought to be excluded from Christian fellowship. In words notably wanting in charity, Evarts wrote that Belsham "as high priest of his order" had access "to the very interior recesses, and has exposed to view the most secret transactions of those, who are initiated into the worship which he approves," and that it is Unitarian strategy "to operate in secret." [15]

While the liberals admittedly did not preach on controverted doctrinal issues, the charge of dishonest concealment was unfair. When Morse sent a copy of his little book to John Adams, the reply of the former President of the United States was prompt and decidedly to the point:

> Sixty-five years ago, my own minister, the Rev. [Lemuel] Bryant, Dr. Jonathan Mayhew, of the West Church in Boston, the Rev. Mr. Shute, of Hingham, the Rev. John Brown, of Cohasset, and perhaps equal to all, if not above all, the Rev. Mr. Gay, of Hingham, were Unitarians.
>
> Among the Laity, how many could I name, Lawyers, Physicians, Tradesmen, Farmers.
>
> More than fifty years ago, I read Dr. Samuel Clark, Emlyn and Dr. Waterland. Do you expect, my dear Doctor, to teach me any thing new in favor of Athanasianism?[16]

Slogans were brought into action; and when Morse asked: "Shall we have the Boston religion, or the Christian religion," John Lowell, another layman ready to defend the honor of the liberal party, replied with a question of his own: "Are you a Christian or a Calvinist?"

The liberals were hurt and angered by the attack launched by Morse and Evarts. The minister of the Federal Street Church, William Ellery Channing, known for his lack of partisan spirit, replied for the liberals. His response was *A Letter to the Rev. Samuel C. Thacher, on the Aspersions Contained in a Late Number of The Panoplist, on the Ministers of Boston and the Vicinity* (1815). In it he rejected out of hand the assertion that the Boston liberals and the English Unitarians were in their theological views indistinguishable. Indeed, he was at pains to show that there was no small diversity of opinion among the liberals. The great majority held a high Arian view, emphasizing that Jesus Christ was more than man, that he came to save the race, and that he is helper and intercessor on our behalf with the Father. At the same time, he acknowledged that there were some who held the Socinian view of the strict humanity of Christ. He freely associated himself with the high Arian view.

The second point Channing felt constrained to make was that Morse and Evarts were unjust in alleging deliberate concealment or hypocrisy regarding their view on the part of the liberal ministers. As for the Trinitarian formula, he said: "We preach precisely as if no such doctrine as the Trinity had ever been known." The liberals had not claimed the Unitarian label because they had no sympathy for sectarian strife of any kind. We speak, he said, of the Father as the one true God, and of Jesus Christ, his son, who yet is distinct from him and subordinate to him. "We have aimed at making no false impression. We have only followed a general system which we are persuaded to be best for our people and for the cause of christianity; the system of excluding controversy as much as possible from our pulpits."[17]

Channing concluded his letter by addressing himself to the harmful results of the sectarian spirit that divides the body of Christ. The call for the orthodox to separate themselves from fellowship with liberals can never serve the interests of truth. The liberals do, indeed, acknowledge "Jesus Christ as our Lord and Master," and are at pains to discover the true meaning of his life as it is set forth in the Gospels, and to order their lives in conformity with his spirit. It is not for these things that division is advocated, but because careful searching of the Scriptures does not support "certain doctrines, which have divided the church for ages." In closing, Channing exhorted his fellow liberals to remain steadfast in their convictions, but to hold to them without rancor, declaring: "Errour of opinion is an evil too trifling to be named in comparison with this practical departure from the Gospel, with this proud, censorious, overbearing temper, which says to a large body of christians, 'stand off, we are holier than you.' " [18]

The orthodox response was now made by Dr. Samuel Worcester of Salem. Worcester maintained that Trinitarian Christianity was the only and necessary way to salvation. Channing asked if the liberals were "unchristian" because they were "untrinitarian." Worcester insisted that the "errours of the Unitarians" were undermining Christianity; Channing insisted that the only scriptural test was belief that "Jesus is the Christ," and that "men of irreproachable character can never do harm to true religion." Three letters from Worcester and two replies from Channing finally brought to a close the second phase of the controversy. The unity of the Standing Order was still maintained by the more irenic spirits, but sides had been drawn, and, tragically, there were unmistakable signs of approaching schism.

Yet even as the liberals protested the "system of exclusion," they were forced to respond by organizing on their own behalf. The decade following the controversy surrounding Ware's election was a time of organizational activity. In 1807, in Lancaster, Massachusetts, the Evangelical Missionary Society was founded by clergy and laymen from Worcester and Middlesex counties, to support work of a religious and moral character in remote parts of New England. There was no distinction of theological opinion imposed for membership, but the catholic spirit of toleration soon made it an enterprise in which the liberals alone participated.

Even earlier a group in the Boston area founded the Society for Promoting Christian Knowledge, Piety, and Charity, and began publishing the *Christian Monitor,* under the editorship of the Reverend William Emerson of the First Church. The society soon expanded its activities by publishing tracts, books, and quarterlies of a devotional character. Before long it was providing study and inspirational materials for the whole family, stressing moral earnestness and a practical, undogmatic Christianity. For more than a century, an authentic piety that was at once evangelical and broadly tolerant was a characteristic aspect of Unitarian faith and life.

At about the same time, under the leadership of John T. Kirkland, steps were taken leading to the organization of the Harvard Divinity School. In 1811, the year following his appointment as president of Harvard, Kirkland assumed responsibility for the instruction of students preparing for the ministry. He himself lectured on Natural and Revealed Religion, while Professor Sidney Willard gave instruction in the Hebrew Scriptures, and Henry Ware introduced students to the criticism of the Greek

New Testament. These three provided the beginnings of a faculty of divinity.

In 1815, the Harvard Corporation approved an appeal for funds, and President Kirkland published an appeal for contributions to provide for financial assistance for divinity students, the appointment of one or more new members of the faculty, and the erection of a building. The appeal brought in some $30,000. In 1816, the subscribers organized the Society for the Promotion of Theological Education, whose purpose was, and has ever since remained, to encourage the "serious, impartial, and unbiased investigation of Christian truth." Samuel Cooper Thacher had attacked the creedal basis on which the orthodox had established Andover, specifically the requirement that professors subscribe to articles of faith, not only at the time of appointment, but thereafter at five-year intervals. It is, then, not surprising that the founders of the Harvard Divinity School should have declared that no assent "to the peculiarities of any denomination of Christians shall be required of the students or instructors." [19]

Kirkland, Channing, and Thacher were named a committee of three to draw up a curriculum, which included instruction by Willard in Hebrew; by Andrews Norton, recently appointed Dexter Lecturer, in Biblical Criticism; and by Dr. Abiel Holmes of the First Church in Cambridge in Ecclesiastical Polity and Church History. Thus the establishment of the Divinity School was accomplished in accordance with the principles of pure, rational, and undogmatic Christianity. For a generation the new Divinity School had the sympathy and support of the liberal party alone, its graduates filling the pulpits of churches that would become Unitarian within two decades; but it steadfastly resisted any compromise with the sectarian temper. This rejection of sectarianism is probably the greatest glory of the liberal spirit, all the more precious for its rarity.

VI

William Ellery Channing was born in Newport, Rhode Island, in 1780. Prepared for college by his uncle, the Reverend Henry Channing of New London, Connecticut, he graduated from Harvard in the class of 1798. As his college years drew to a close,

Channing had not yet settled on a future course for his life. For two years he was tutor in a private family in Richmond, Virginia, a period marked by much study, introspection, and spiritual anxiety. After a time in Newport, Channing was once again in Cambridge for the opening of the college in 1802, having determined to read for the ministry. In 1803, he was ordained and installed as minister of the Federal Street Church, where he remained for the rest of his life.

Channing was not easily drawn into theological controversy, and he seems to have maintained a middle position in the debate that grew in intensity in the early years of his ministry. Yet, years later, Channing said that there was a time when he had tended toward the Calvinistic position, but the doctrine of the Trinity stood in the way. He had never been, he said, in any sense whatever a Trinitarian. If others were for division, Channing wanted unity. But when, in 1815, Morse and Evarts charged the liberals with deliberate concealment of their true views, Channing, as we have seen, was too deeply stirred to remain silent.

For three years, the arguments rested. Then the liberals were ready to take the initiative, and this time to carry the debate outside Boston. In 1818, Dr. Freeman journeyed to Baltimore to preach at the dedication of the newly erected Unitarian church, declared by some to be the handsomest church building in America. It was not his first visit. Two years earlier, he had preached in Baltimore on three occasions, with the result that a Unitarian congregation had been gathered in that city "for the maintenance of Unitarian and anti-Calvinistic worship." Now the congregation with its fine new building was ready to settle a minister, and the choice for that position was Jared Sparks, a young Harvard graduate. Between his call and settlement, the Baltimore church had as its interim minister none other than Harvard's President, John Thornton Kirkland!

Channing had been young Sparks's mentor, and to him went the invitation to deliver the sermon of ordination. It has been called the most famous sermon ever delivered in America. That the occasion was carefully planned to provide a powerful statement in defense of "pure and rational Christianity" is abundantly clear when one surveys the list of participants. There was Dr. Nathaniel Thayer of Lancaster, "a veritable Nestor among the

Joseph Stevens Buckminster

Henry Ware, Sr.

William Ellery Channing

Liberals of New England," Dr. Eliphalet Porter of Roxbury, a
Fellow of Harvard, and Dr. Ware, the Hollis Professor. These
were "the three pillar apostles of the Council." Then there was
Nathan Parker of Portsmouth, New Hampshire, a distinguished
minister and very popular with the students of Exeter Academy;
Henry Edes of Providence, noted for his preaching and his
prayers; and Ichabod Nichols of the First Church in Portland,
Maine, where he served for 49 years. Finally, there was John G.
Palfrey, Sparks's friend and classmate, later to be dean of the
Divinity School, and Channing himself.[20]

The ordination of Sparks on May 5, 1819, was the occasion for
Channing's great manifesto, which he called simply: "Unitarian
Christianity." It has been described with some justification as the
"Pentecost of American Unitarianism." Taking some ninety minutes to deliver the sermon, Channing defined the issues that
united the liberals and distinguished their views from commonly-
held orthodox opinions. It was a powerful statement of principles.

He began with a careful and clear exposition of the nature of
Scripture, and, most important, of the methods to be used in the
study of the Bible. The Bible is a record of God's successive revela-
tions to mankind, but not all its parts are equally important. The
New Testament is more important than the Old, and Jesus'
teachings more than other parts of the New Testament. It is not
the Scriptures that are inspired, but it is inspired men and women
whom we encounter in the Scriptures. And, echoing Buckminster,
he declared that the meaning of the Bible "is to be sought in the
same manner as that of other books." Scripture contains revelation, but it must be interpreted by reason, for "Revelation is
addressed to us as rational beings." The Bible must be harmonized
with the will of God, and "with the obvious and acknowledged
laws of nature." Here Channing was moving the discussion onto
new ground. By earlier New England liberals, like Charles
Chauncy, the Bible had been considered to be its own sufficient
interpreter, the obscure passages being clarified by the unam-
biguous ones. Now an external source of authority was acknowledged—the laws of nature—and reason was the instrument for its
validation.[21]

Having set forth the principles of criticism, Channing went on to show what Scripture, rightly understood, teaches. First he declared that it clearly proclaims the unity of God: "we believe in the doctrine of God's *unity*. . . . We understand by it, that there is one being, one mind, one person. . . . We object to the doctrine of the Trinity, that, whilst acknowledging in words, it subverts in effect, the unity of God." [22]

Secondly, he affirmed the unity of Christ, as possessing one nature, not two—a divine nature as part of the Godhead, and a human nature. Examine the passages in Scripture, Channing declared, in which Jesus is distinguished from God, and you will find "that they not only speak of him as another being, but seem to labor to express his inferiority." [23]

The third point was, for Channing, the most significant: "We believe in the *moral perfection of God*." The almighty power of God is "submitted to his perception of rectitude"; his goodness is infinite; and his justice and mercy make blasphemous the doctrines of human depravity, the perversion of the will, and eternal damnation. Here, for Channing, was the very heart of his difference with Calvinism.

His fourth point had to do with the mediation of Christ. Christ was surely not sent to appease God, but, rather, he "was sent by that mercy, to be our Saviour." It is the moral example of Christ that reveals to us the way of reconciliation with the Father: "he was sent by the Father to effect a moral, or spiritual deliverance of mankind. . . ." [24]

Finally, Channing turned to the nature of true holiness, which is to be seen in one's love to God, love to Christ, and love toward one's fellows.

The response to Channing's sermon was immediate. It has been asserted that its circulation exceeded that of any other American publication up to that time, save only Tom Paine's *Common Sense*. Five editions were printed in six weeks. Translated into several languages and steadily reissued, it stands as one of the great sermons of the American church. If the orthodox reaction was hardly enthusiastic, the liberals, now on the offensive, were jubilant.

The most significant criticism directed at the sermon came from Moses Stuart, Andover's leading biblical scholar. Stuart, who had acquired at auction some volumes from Buckminster's library, had hoped that biblical criticism would be the bridge between the two parties within Congregationalism. He had shared books and ideas with Edward Everett, Buckminster's successor, as they worked their way into the new criticism through Eichhorn's *Einleitung*. That coveted volume was one of those purchased by Stuart at the Buckminster auction. By 1819, Stuart had a good knowledge of biblical criticism, but he was at heart a theologian, not a historian. He held to the unity of the Bible, and had no real sense of the significance of the critical methodology that located the biblical books in the context, age, and world-view of their authors. These matters were, of course, basic considerations for Channing.

Stuart responded to Channing's sermon in his *Letters to the Rev. Wm. E. Channing, Containing Remarks on His Sermon*. He expressed agreement for the most part with Channing's principles of interpretation, but took issue with his way of presenting the orthodox view of the Trinity. At the same time, he admitted that he, himself, did not fully understand the philosophical language in which the doctrine was couched. The task of responding to Stuart's *Letters* was assumed by Andrews Norton, since 1813 Dexter Lecturer on Biblical Criticism, who had just been named Professor of Sacred Literature at the Divinity School. Norton had taken a position in the forefront of theological debate as early as 1812, when he became editor of the *General Respository and Review*. In touch with the new biblical criticism, he insisted that the issues it raised not be ignored and that reason be used in discovering the meaning of Scripture; and he vigorously articulated the most advanced views of biblical authority, locating inspiration not in the Scriptures but in the men who produced them. This method, he believed, would enable thoughtful persons to recover pure Christianity.

Norton wrote two review articles on the Baltimore Sermon. The first centered on Christology and on the methods used in interpreting Scripture. The second was destined to have a wide influence both on the immediate debate and in setting new directions for the next phase of the controversy. It was soon printed as a pamphlet under the title: *A Statement of Reasons for Not Believing the Doctrines of Trinitarians Respecting the Nature of God, and the Person of Christ*. It appeared in 1819, and a much expanded version of it in 1833. With Norton's new thrust, the debate moved from the issues of methodology and biblical inspiration to the theological questions involved in the doctrine of the Trinity. If the older generation of liberals had not cared to engage in theological disputation, Andrews Norton was of a different cut; he saw where the debate was going and led the way. His *Statement of Reasons* and Stuart's *Letters to Channing* exposed to full view the confusion that existed in the orthodox ranks over the language and meaning of the doctrine of the Trinity.[25]

The discussion now moved to the contrasting liberal and orthodox views of human nature. Professor Leonard Woods of Andover and Professor Henry Ware of Harvard stepped forward to defend their respective parties. For three years they carried on a polite and scholarly exchange, long ago dubbed, by those who looked on, "the Wood 'n Ware Controversy." When it drew to a close in 1822, the debate was found to have run to some 800 pages. If no issues were resolved, the distinctions between the two branches of Congregationalism were projected in sharp relief.[26]

VII

Meanwhile, the next phase of the controversy leading to separation was already under way. It was not concerned directly with theological issues, but with a set of questions regarding church organization, and the rights of the majority in ecclesiastical matters. It was the knotty problem of the relationship of the church to the parish in the peculiar structures of congregational polity.

Congregationalism is not a system of doctrine, but a pattern of ecclesiastical organization by which authority to exercise rule over the church resides in the congregation itself. Originally in New England Congregationalism, membership in the church was restricted to "saints by calling"—that is to say, those who may be presumed to have been elected by God in accordance with his eternal decrees. The test of a true church, then, is a gathered congregation voluntarily covenanted under the rule of Christ, the Church's true head. Every congregation so constituted is a church, whole and entire, empowered to choose its officers, call and ordain its own minister, and administer its own affairs without outside hierarchical control.

But for the Puritans, religion was not a matter of concern only to those who were presumed to be of the elect and admitted to the communion table. Religious values permeated the whole society, and were shared by elect and non-elect alike. Indeed, the New England Puritans thought of themselves as an elect nation, the whole community being in covenant with God, and their earthly prosperity dependent on their doing his will, supporting public worship, and maintaining the ordinances in all purity. Hence responsibility for the public worship of God—the costs of maintaining the meeting house and the salary of the minister— was a common responsibility of all the inhabitants of each town, not just a matter for the select body of church members.

As long as the society was relatively homogeneous, no serious problem arose. But in the course of the eighteenth century, the society became more and more secularized, and religious pluralism increased as Baptists, Quakers, and Anglicans intruded beside the churches of the Standing Order. The possibilities for disagreement between the Congregational church and the town (or parish) increased. If the inhabitants of the town were to be taxed for the support of the minister, should they not have a say in his selection? But what then became of the independence of the church to order its own affairs under the rule of the Lord Jesus Christ? In 1693, in Massachusetts, it was provided by law that the church should choose and the town concur; but what if the two could not agree?

After the outbreak of the Unitarian Controversy, the church members in many communities tended to be theologically more orthodox or evangelical than the inhabitants at large of the town or parish. When a vacancy in the pulpit was to be filled, the members of the parish might well favor a liberal; while the orthodox majority of the small company of church members was becoming increasingly less willing to accept any one who did not adhere to traditional Westminster standards. "Can two walk together, except they be agreed?" they asked; and they responded by severing their connection with the territorial parish.

It seemed only plausible to the members of a Congregational church that took this step by majority vote that it continued to be the same covenanted body as before. It gave up all privileges derived from association with a territorial parish, such as tax support for the ministry; but it surely was entitled to retain its records and such properties as had been given to the church, as distinct from the parish, such as communion silver and charitable funds. By Province laws, its deacons had been made a body corporate in order to hold title to such property. But in a famous decision handed down in February, 1821, the courts rejected that line of argument, stating rather that in Massachusetts law a Congregational church existed only in relationship to a town, parish, precinct, or religious society. The cries of outrage on the part of the orthodox were shrill, and relations between the orthodox and the liberals were embittered to such a degree that in some communities the scars still remain, even though five generations have passed.

The decision of the court was in the case of *Baker v. Fales,* commonly referred to as the "Dedham Case." In 1818, the First Parish in Dedham chose Alvan Lamson as its "public teacher of piety, religion, and morality," to replace the Reverend Joshua Bates, who had resigned. The choice was not acceptable to a majority of the church members, who subsequently withdrew, taking with them the records and the communion plate. The minority of the church remaining argued in effect that those who departed thereby became uncovenanted individuals, and that the continuity of the covenanted church body rested with the faithful few who stayed behind. They elected new deacons to take the place of those who had departed, who entered suit for recovery of the church property. They were upheld by the Supreme Judicial Court, whose position was summarized in the Massachusetts Reports thus: "When a majority of the members of a Congregational church separate from a majority of the parish, the members who remain, although a minority, constitute the church in such parish, and retain the rights and property belonging thereto." [27]

Within a few years, the break in the Standing Order was complete. According to a tabulation prepared by the orthodox in 1836, in at least 81 cases, it was their members who were "exiled." [28] The number of instances in which the liberals rather than the orthodox withdrew was much smaller, amounting to a dozen or more. In addition, there were more than a score of churches which moved into the liberal camp without dispute or division. When the period of controversy was over, about one-third of the Congregational churches of Massachusetts had become Unitarian. Among them was a high proportion of the oldest and wealthiest, their membership including many of the leading decision-makers of the community. The assessment of the situation by the orthodox party was well expressed by Harriet Beecher Stowe, as she recalled the arrival of her father in Boston in 1826:

When Dr. Beecher came to Boston, Calvinism or orthodoxy was the despised and persecuted form of faith. It was the dethroned royal family wandering like a permitted mendicant in the city where once it had held court, and Unitarianism reigned in its stead.

All the literary men of Massachusetts were Unitarian. All the trustees and professors of Harvard College were Unitarians. All the élite of wealth and fashion crowded Unitarian churches. The judges on the bench were Unitarian, giving decisions by which the peculiar features of church organization, so carefully ordained by the Pilgrim fathers, had been nullified. The Church, as consisting, according to their belief, in regenerate people, had been ignored, and all the power had passed into the hands of the congregation.[29]

Divinity Hall at Harvard

VIII

By 1820, there were some 120 Unitarian churches in eastern Massachusetts, and another ten in the other New England states. Five years later, nine churches in Maine were avowedly Unitarian. On his way to Baltimore, Channing had stopped in New York City to preach in a private home to a small group gathered for the occasion. Henry Ware, Jr., had preached there the year before. On the return from Baltimore, services were again held, with several of the New England leaders preaching. The First Congregational Church, now All Souls, was gathered later that year.[30] Philadelphia, Charleston, and Washington now had Unitarian congregations as well.

The question that confronted the liberal party next was one of organization. Sentiment for preserving the unity of the Congregational church order was still strong among many of the leading laymen and clergy, although *de facto* separation was increasingly evident. On May 30, 1820 (the time of the annual election being by tradition the occasion for ministerial gatherings), Channing invited the liberal ministers to meet at the Federal Street Church to consider some kind of organization, and urged an organization of liberal clergymen for mutual encouragement. "It was thought by some of us," he said, "that the ministers of this commonwealth who are known to agree in what are called liberal or catholic views of Christianity needed a bond of union, a means of intercourse, and an opportunity of conference not as yet enjoyed." [31] Thus the Berry Street Conference came into being; and it has provided through the years some of the very benefits Channing hoped it might.

The following year, the Publishing Fund Society was founded by liberal ministers and laymen "desirous of promoting the circulation of works adapted to improve the public mind in religion and morality." The founders were explicit in their refusal to support any sectarian effort, preferring instead to produce materials devoted to the nurturing of a practical Christian morality in the young people, and to provide devotional materials for adults. The lack of sectarian zeal, surely widespread among the liberals, was fully visible in efforts of this sort.

There were young men, though, who were impatient for some form of denominational organization. In 1824, the Anonymous Association, an informal group of some of the leading men of Boston, heard Channing discuss the feasibility of forming a Unitarian convention or association. The discussion led to the naming of a committee, charged with planning a larger meeting for purposes of exploring the question of an association. The meeting was held with some 44 interested ministers and laymen in attendance.[32]

Students and recent graduates of the Divinity School, who had the support and encouragement of Professor Andrews Norton, were eager for organization; but opposition was sufficiently strong that a proposed larger meeting for further discussion was, in fact, never held. Three young ministers, however, pushed forward with a plan. James Walker, Henry Ware, Jr., and Ezra Stiles Gannett presented a proposal to the Berry Street Conference at its next meeting; and the following day, May 26, 1825, a constitution for the American Unitarian Association was adopted, defining the purposes of the new organization to be "to diffuse the knowledge and promote the interests of pure Christianity." The separation of the two branches of Congregationalism was now institutionalized, and there was no turning back.

When the founders of the new association named William Ellery Channing as their choice for president, they found him unwilling to accept. He appeared to be surprised at what seemed to him to be precipitous action in launching the new organization; yet, in his letter to Gannett declining the office, he wrote: "As you have made a beginning, I truly rejoice in your success." Aaron Bancroft, an elder statesman of the liberal cause, and since 1786 the widely respected minister of the Second Church in Worcester, became the first president of the American Unitarian Association. He held the office for a decade, retiring in 1835 at the age of eighty.

The burden of executive responsibility fell on Ezra Stiles Gannett, the Association's first secretary. If the elder men feared sectarianism, Gannett, catholic in his sympathies, was nevertheless fervently committed to the cause of restoring historic Christianity to its first purity. It was a spirit and a hope that was fully shared by his fellow laborers. The Executive Committee, beginning work

at once, drew up a statement of purposes in one of its first meetings. With a view to promoting "the great doctrines and principles in which all Christians coincide," they would seek "to
diffuse the knowledge and influence of the gospel of our Lord and
Saviour." [33]

Support for the new association was slow in coming, but the
decade from 1825 to 1835 was, nevertheless, one of steady growth.
The oldest churches were deeply committed to principles of
mutual freedom and independence, and that commitment ran too
deep to make uniting for action a thing easily accomplished. The
creation of a more cohesive movement was the task of another
generation. Yet the spirituality that these churches cultivated, and
the ethical and moral earnestness that led to a remarkable age of
philanthropy and social concern, are a precious heritage from
those who listened to the words of Freeman, Channing, Norton,
and all the others who proclaimed the gospel of pure and rational
Christianity. Lack of sectarian temper is part of that heritage, too.
In a letter to a friend, Channing wrote:

> I distrust sectarian influence more and more. I am more detached
> from a denomination, and strive to feel more my connection with the
> Universal Church, with all good and holy men. I am little a Uni-
> tarian, and stand aloof from all but those who strive and pray for
> clearer light, who look for a purer and more effective manifestation
> of Christian truth.[34]

It was easy for the next generation to denigrate the religion of
Channing's day, with its commitment to a religion based on
reason, and to describe it, albeit unfairly, as "corpse-cold." But
Unitarianism in its first period displayed a remarkable combination of catholicity, authentic piety, and practical morality. It was
a splendid achievement.

Chapter 2

"At Morning Blest
and Golden-Browed"

*Unitarians, Transcendentalists,
and Reformers, 1835-1865*

The era from 1835 to 1865 might well be called "the golden age" of American Unitarianism. Boston and its nearby towns, where the young denomination remained centered, nurtured the most intellectually exciting life in the country at the time. There the major publishing houses were located; there the most adventurous philosophical and spiritual speculation in the United States went on; there the most advanced social reform projects were proposed. To all this activity Unitarianism contributed in ways that were important, probably even indispensable. Organized religion and religious currents of thought exerted a compelling power in shaping the outlook of Americans during the years culminating in the Civil War. Most aspects of culture—including education, literature, politics, and reform—were intimately bound up with religion; and Unitarian religion seems to have provided a powerful stimulus for innovative thought and action in the period to which we now turn.

After 1835 Unitarians found themselves no longer so involved in debating theological issues against other Protestant groups. The chief explanation for this lies in the gradual loss of dedication to Calvinist rigor on the part of the orthodox. The principal Trinitarian spokesmen of the mid-nineteenth century and later, Horace Bushnell, Phillips Brooks, and Henry Ward Beecher, were ecumenical-minded theological moderates. Their views on predestination, atonement, and original sin actually had less in common with their orthodox predecessors than with their Unitarian contemporaries. Slowly adopting many attitudes that were more or less liberal themselves, such churchmen did not share Jedidiah Morse's determination to expose heresy and root it out. Since most Unitarians had never found the controversies very congenial, when their adversaries lost interest they were only too happy to discontinue them. The disestablishment of religion in Massachusetts removed the principal occasion for disputes over property, such as the one at Dedham. Other issues seemed more pressing, concerns that were to remain of central importance to Unitarians until the present day. One of these was how to implement liberal religion in the world. The other was the quest for its proper philosophical foundation.

I

"Now that we are a community by ourselves, it behooves us to consider what we shall do," Henry Ware, Jr., told his fellow Unitarians in 1835.[1] Among the secular activities reflecting Unitarian religious commitments were many relating to the promotion of literacy and learning. A religion teaching that people should think for themselves, Unitarianism accorded an important place to education. New Englanders had a long tradition of support for the common schools, but the Unitarians of the middle third of the nineteenth century were remarkable even among Yankees for their devotion to education. The younger Ware called education "the business of life." The proper development of one's talents and potential was a duty to God as well as to oneself, he asserted; a well-rounded liberal education was not a mere ornament for the well-to-do, but a necessity for every person.[2] William Ellery Channing and the other prominent Unitarian clergy concurred fully with Ware. All human powers ("faculties," as they were termed) required careful training if they were to fulfill the purpose God intended. It is no exaggeration to say that such Unitarian religious leaders considered the school as sacred an institution as the church. After the end of public support for the churches in 1833, it became more important than ever that public support for education be put on an effective basis.[3]

The most famous of Unitarian educational reformers was Horace Mann. Converted to Unitarianism from orthodoxy by Channing, Mann put into practice the doctrines he learned from the great preacher of Federal Street. "If republican institutions wake up unexampled energies in the whole mass of a people," Mann insisted, "these same institutions ought also to confer upon that people unexampled wisdom and rectitude." [4] Mann served as secretary of the Massachusetts Board of Education from 1837 to 1848, during which time he virtually created the first statewide system of public schools and the first teachers' college (at Lexington in 1839) in the United States. He sought not only to rationalize educational administration and improve teaching, but also to restrict religious instruction in the schools to a nonsectarian core of principles common to all Protestants. The orthodox, accustomed to prescribing Calvinist tenets in many public schools, complained that Mann's "nonsectarian" principles were equivalent to Unitarianism. Mann, like most Massachusetts Unitarians of his time, was a member of the Whig party; hence he met with partisan opposition from Democrats. The debates over Mann's educational reforms show how religious rivalries carried over into politics.[5] In many ways, indeed, social, cultural, and political controversy replaced theological controversy as arenas of competition between Unitarians and others after 1835.

Besides Horace Mann's school system, a host of other institutions for the promotion of learning flourished under predominantly Unitarian auspices in mid-nineteenth-century Massachusetts. The Library of the Boston Athenaeum (founded in 1807), the Lowell Institute (founded in 1836), and the Boston Public Library (founded in 1854) are among the best known of many. The Athenaeum's facilities were used by a rather select clientele, but most of the other institutions served a wider public. The endowment of these institutions by affluent Unitarian laymen shows that the injunctions of Unitarian clergy regarding the importance of learning were taken seriously and heeded. The organization and support of the institutions served a social function as well as an intellectual one. Their interlocking network, along with Harvard University and the Unitarian churches, knit the business and professional families of Boston together, giving them a sense of common purpose and identity.[6]

Of course Harvard continued to be the most important center of Unitarian learning. The composition of the faculty, to be sure, was not exclusive: at one point in the 1830s the staff of fourteen included, along with six Unitarians, three Roman Catholics, a Calvinist, a Lutheran, an Episcopalian, a Quaker, and a "Sandemanian." [7] Despite such attempts at ecumenicity, however, Harvard remained in the public mind a Unitarian academy, and not without reason. The Divinity School was uniformly Unitarian in point of view and student body, and the presidents of the university throughout this period were all Unitarians.[8] When Frederic Dan Huntington, Plummer Professor of Christian Morals in the College, converted from Unitarianism to the Episcopal church in 1860, he felt constrained to resign his chair. Since Harvard was still in some respects affiliated with the Commonwealth of Massachusetts, non-Unitarian citizens, especially the staunch Calvinists, resented all this. Identification with Unitarianism exposed the university to harassment from Democratic politicians in Massachusetts, who courted Calvinist votes by denouncing Harvard or even by interfering with its academic freedom (in 1851 the Democratic politicians on the Board of Overseers denied a professorship to an especially outspoken Unitarian Whig). The problem was relieved as Harvard gradually eliminated its ties to the government of the Commonwealth, until by 1865 it had become a totally private university.[9]

The curriculum at Harvard College was intended to provide a liberal education that would develop the moral and intellectual powers of the student. This educational objective was typical of most institutions of higher learning in the Western world, but nowhere else was the development of human potential invested with such religious significance. The capstone of the curriculum was a course in moral philosophy, usually taken in the senior year. "Moral philosophy," as it was then broadly defined, included the application as well as the theory of value judgments; thus it treated all of what we consider the social sciences and even literary criticism, as well as abstract ethics. The moral philosophy taught at Harvard had largely been created by Arminian philosophers in Scotland during the eighteenth century. While Scottish moral philosophy was also taught at "orthodox" religious colleges in the United States, its emphasis on human morality and human ability synthesized more readily with Unitarian than Calvinistic theology. At Harvard, Scottish moral philosophy and liberal Christianity provided a comprehensive and integrated world-view centered on the proper cultivation of human nature.[10]

Unitarianism came to exert more influence in America through its humanistic and cultural concerns than through sectarian proselytizing. The Boston *Monthly Anthology* of Joseph Stevens Buckminster and his friends (published 1803-1811) had shown how literature could substitute for theology as a means of moral influence.[11] William Ellery Channing's essay on "National Literature" (1830) exhorted Americans to define themselves as a people through the creation of a body of writing expressing their ideals.[12] The minister's brother, Edward Tyrell Channing, professor of oratory and rhetoric at Harvard from 1819 to 1852, did much to achieve this end by training many students who later became leading writers of the New England literary "renaissance." The principal Unitarian magazine between 1824 and 1869, the *Christian Examiner,* displayed a "broad and catholic" taste in belles lettres as well as religion, while the more famous *North American Review* conveyed predominantly Unitarian views on a variety of subjects to the general reading public.

This highly literate New England Unitarianism produced a disproportionate number of America's writers and scholars during the period before the Civil War. Among them were George Ticknor, first professor of modern foreign languages in the United States, and the narrative historians William Hickling Prescott and John Lothrop Motley. All three wrote on the rise and fall of the Spanish empire, a subject that fascinated them because of the moral lessons they drew from it, lessons vindicating their own nineteenth-century liberalism in politics and religion. Through their monumental studies of the evils that brought Catholic, autocratic Spain to ruin, Ticknor, Prescott, and Motley applied the ethical ideals of Unitarianism, as they understood them, to history.[13]

Even more widely read than the Unitarian historians were the classic Unitarian poets: Oliver Wendell Holmes the elder, William Cullen Bryant, James Russell Lowell, and Henry Wadsworth Longfellow. Their work has become such an integral part of our heritage that, together with the Quaker John Greenleaf Whittier, they are often called the "household poets." Holmes's love for Harvard and dislike for Calvinism both come out in his poetry.

His satire "The Deacon's Masterpiece" (1858), in which a wonderful "one-hoss shay" falls apart just as Holmes believed Calvinist theology had done, was probably the most effective retort (on a popular level) to the logic of orthodox dogma Unitarians ever produced.[14] Bryant, one of the few Unitarians of this period to belong to the Democratic rather than the Whig party, combined his gift for enduring verse with a career as editor of the New York *Evening Post*. Lowell consecrated much of his poetic talent to propagandizing against slavery, since it was axiomatic among Unitarians of his generation that art should serve the cause of social morality and righteousness. Like Lowell and George Ticknor, Longfellow taught Romance languages at Harvard for part of his career. In his lifetime Longfellow was the best-loved poet in the English language, but in the twentieth century literary critics have sometimes treated him with unwarranted contempt. His poems provide a gold mine for anyone exploring the Unitarian mind; their calmness, sense of human dignity, and appreciation for nature endure even though their didacticism and sentimentality now seem quaint. The Unitarian poets transcended the limits of their numerically small denomination to transmit the values of liberal religion to the largest possible audience.[15]

II

Unitarians sought to put their religion into practice in many other spheres besides education and literature during the generation before the Civil War. Nineteenth-century Unitarians were probably the most convinced believers in progress the world has ever known, and many of them were eager to help in the improvement of mankind that God willed. Prison reform, the founding of orphanages, the abolition of dueling and of capital punishment —these and other causes found favor among many Liberal Christians. The peace movement, pioneered by Noah Worcester (Unitarian brother of the Calvinist who debated Channing), took on renewed life during the Mexican War, which was intensely unpopular among Unitarians and most other northern Whigs. Temperance, especially during its early phases when it literally espoused moderation in the use of alcohol, rather than prohibition, did not lack Unitarian advocates. Certain crusades of the time, like sabbatarianism and missions, were so closely identified with evangelical orthodoxy that Unitarians participated little in them. But in humanitarian philanthropy and reform, it would be hard for any other denomination, even the Quakers, to equal the record of Unitarianism in mid-nineteenth-century America.

Because of the emphasis of the Unitarians on human dignity, it was fitting that they should contribute two of the greatest crusaders on behalf of the handicapped: Samuel Gridley Howe and Dorothea Dix. Howe served as director of the New England Asylum for the Blind from 1829 to 1873; Dix began in 1843 a crusade for the establishment of asylums for the mentally ill that achieved remarkable success not only in the northern states but in the South and Europe as well. Howe's work in training the blind and Dix's with the retarded and disturbed complemented that of their friend Horace Mann in educating normal children. Even more than he, they were impelled by a vision of human perfectibility. No matter how disadvantaged or seemingly limited, every human being was designed by God for indefinite improvement, Unitarian ministers like Channing and Ware preached, and the achievements of Samuel Gridley Howe and Dorothea Dix were built upon this faith.

One of the most interesting social causes undertaken by Unitarians before the Civil War was the ministry to the poor of Boston. This was initiated by the American Unitarian Association in 1826, the year after its founding. Joseph Tuckerman, previously minister of the church in Chelsea, answered the call. He styled himself "minister-at-large" to the city, and concerned himself with the temporal, as well as spiritual, welfare of the urban poor. His first chapel was a room above a warehouse. With financial backing from the A.U.A. supplemented by donations from well-wishers, Tuckerman was able to set up a farm school outside the city to rehabilitate juvenile delinquents and a sewing school to help young girls in the black community get jobs. He also made grants—more often loans—to individuals. His practice of visiting troubled families in their homes and discussing their problems has caused Tuckerman to be considered a pioneer social worker.[16]

Tuckerman accounted carefully to his sponsors with semiannual reports describing both the conditions of poverty he encountered and the methods through which he sought to cope with them. An examination of the reports reveals the limitations as well as the aspirations of his old-fashioned philanthropy.[17] Tuckerman firmly opposed the unionization of labor and all government activity on behalf of social justice, believing that private charity could handle problems more effectively. He considered the material well-being of his clients as a means to improving their spiritual condition, rather than as an end in itself, though he defined "spiritual condition" broadly. Like so many other Unitarians of his day, Tuckerman proved an effective organizer: in 1834, with encouragement from Ezra Stiles Gannett and the younger Ware, nine Boston Unitarian parishes formed a Benevolent Fraternity of Churches for the support of the ministry-at-large. By 1838 other denominations had entered the enterprise, and there were ten ministers to the poor of the city, of whom four were Unitarians. One of the first people to try to awaken the American bourgeoisie to the plight of the urban lower class, Tuckerman was clearly a precursor of what later became known as the "social gospel."

Of all the humanitarian efforts of the mid-nineteenth century, none occasioned more anguish and internal strife among Unitarians than the crusade against slavery. Slavery was, of course, the ultimate denial of Christian humanism—the doctrine, which Unitarians emphasized, that "a *man*, be his nation, complexion, condition, or capacity what it may, is an image of God." [18] The same dedication to developing human potential which impelled Unitarians to foster education also dictated opposition to slavery. In theory Unitarians were quite clear that religion confirmed the Declaration of Independence: "all men are created equal." Conduct sometimes fell short of principle, for a variety of reasons. Some of the most prominent Unitarian laymen, such as the Appletons and the Lowells, were textile-mill owners, members of an agricultural-industrial complex that felt threatened by attacks on the southern cotton planters and their mode of production. Thus antislavery had more profoundly disturbing social consequences than other contemporary reform movements.

Unitarians in politics found the slavery question pitting them against each other. President Millard Fillmore and the eloquent Daniel Webster proved willing to compromise with the South in hopes of preserving the Union. Governor Edward Everett, having turned from the ministry and scholarship to a succession of high political offices, followed Webster's lead. Other Unitarian political leaders, however, were strong in the cause of freedom. Former President John Quincy Adams, who served in the federal House of Representatives from 1831 to 1848, vigorously championed the civil liberties of abolitionists whom the South tried to silence. Charles Sumner, a close friend of William Ellery Channing and later senator from Massachusetts, denounced not only "the barbarism of slavery" in the South but also racial segregation in the North.[19] During the 1840s the rivalry between Webster-Everett moderates and the more militantly antislavery group became so marked they earned the respective names "cotton" Whigs and "conscience" Whigs. Finally, in the 1850s, the Whig party to which most Unitarians had belonged disintegrated altogether under the pressures of continued disagreement. Because the Unitarians of this generation were such a closely knit community, they keenly regretted the divisions among them engendered by the slavery issue.

The Unitarian clergy, like the politicians, felt conflicting pressures. As moral leaders of their people, the clergy acknowledged a duty to stand up and be counted on a moral issue. On the other hand, to speak out strongly against slavery did not come easily. Few Unitarian ministers were temperamentally combative men; many were no more inclined to rush into controversy with slaveholders and their northern apologists than they had been to attack the Calvinists. Most ministers considered themselves primarily pastors rather than social critics, and wondered how hard they could press their congregations on a matter where there was no consensus. The records of Unitarian clergymen in the North on slavery vary from abstract disapproval coupled with practical acquiescence all the way to the most dedicated devotion to abolition. The few Unitarian ministers in the South usually tried to avoid the subject.[20]

Two clerical exemplars of "cotton" Whiggery were Orville Dewey, minister of the Church of the Messiah in New York City from 1835 to 1848, and Ezra Stiles Gannett, assistant and successor to Channing at the Federal Street Church (which became the Arlington Street Church in 1859). Dewey admitted that "it cannot possibly be right to hold down and bind to earth the faculties of an immortal creature" in bondage; Gannett went so far as to call slavery "the greatest evil under which our nation labors." [21] Both men believed the best ultimate solution lay in sending American blacks to Africa. When it became clear that colonization was not a viable solution, neither found an effective alternative mode of opposition to slavery. Dewey and Gannett went along with Webster in supporting the Compromise of 1850, including its Fugitive Slave Law, as regrettable but necessary to keep the Union intact. "I would consent that my own brother, my own son, should go" into slavery rather than sacrifice the Union, Dewey emphatically declared. However, when extradition of the fugitive Anthony Burns from Massachusetts to Virginia in 1854 provoked riots and required two thousand troops to enforce, Gannett could bear it no longer. "The Union may cost too much," he concluded ruefully.[22] Mounting tensions and violence brought out differences between the two moderates. Dewey gradually became more solidly northern in sympathies and justified a "holy war" to preserve the Union after all attempts to placate the South had failed. Gannett, however, did not relish the war or urge support of it except by denouncing the New York City anti-draft riots.

Probably the most influential leadership against slavery to come from the Unitarian clergy was provided by William Ellery Channing. A person of refined sensibilities, Channing had initially been put off by the abolitionists' "piercing tones of passion." Apparently these reminded him too much of the methods of itinerant revivalists, which religious liberals had deplored for generations.[23] Channing was persuaded to enter the lists on behalf of freedom by the example of John Quincy Adams and the urgings of a tactful Unitarian abolitionist, Samuel J. May. In 1835 Channing published a short book, *Slavery,* which summed up effectively the ethical argument against the institution. More than that, it carefully considered the consquences of emancipation, advocating that the government assume the cost of both compensating slaveowners and educating the freedmen. (In this respect Channing distinguished himself from the abolitionists proper, who were unwilling to see compensation paid for ending a sin.) Almost forgotten today, Channing's *Slavery* remains one of the clearest and most judicious treatments of its subject ever written by an American.

Despite its careful calm, however, Channing's discussion of

slavery encountered angry denunciations from southerners and even some resentment among Channing's own congregation. James T. Austin, attorney general of Massachusetts and one of Channing's parishioners, accused his minister of inciting race war.[24] In 1840 the Federal Street Standing Committee refused permission for a memorial service to be held for their minister's friend Karl Follen (a distinguished German emigré who had taught at Harvard and become a Unitarian minister) because of the latter's antislavery sentiments. Channing, by then in semi-retirement, was wounded by this insensitivity of the people he had served so long. Though Ezra Gannett loyally supported Channing's request in this matter, one suspects there were members of the congregation who found Gannett's generally conservative views a relief after his great predecessor died in 1842.

Another variant of clerical moral leadership is illustrated by John Gorham Palfrey. Palfrey had spent twelve years as minister to the Church in Brattle Square and five years as dean of Harvard Divinity School when he decided to try his hand at journalism by becoming editor and owner of the *North American Review* in 1835. Eventually he resigned the deanship (1839) and resolved to follow the example of Edward Everett by entering politics. During 1842 and '43 he served annual terms in the Massachusetts General Court (legislature), where he supported the educational reforms of Horace Mann. Palfrey went on to become secretary of state for the Commonwealth, and in 1846 was elected to Congress. There he quickly established himself as an opponent of Everett's moderation and a member of a small band of determined and resourceful "conscience" Whigs. Palfrey's credentials as an advocate of freedom were the more impressive for his having manumitted, when he could ill afford it financially, twenty slaves he inherited, whom he brought north and helped to find jobs.[25] His political activity did not prevent this versatile man from establishing reputations as a biblical scholar and a historian of colonial New England. It was a fitting compliment when, in 1865, the American Unitarian Association elected Palfrey its president.

III

The application of moral concern to the world through reform was not the only important set of religious problems with which Unitarians grappled during the eventful thirty years before 1865. The other was, in a way, even more fundamental; it dealt with the very question of what religion is all about. The matter at issue was this: should religion—specifically, liberal religion—be ultimately rational? The conventional Unitarian answer had been an emphatic "Yes." Then a "New School" of religious liberals called Transcendentalists began to insist otherwise. Religion, they proclaimed, was properly a matter of intuition, emotion, and faith. In the highly sensitive and articulate Unitarian community of the 1830s and '40s, this dispute attracted wider attention than we today can readily imagine. Passions ran high, and for a time the split threatened to become permanent. Though some Transcendentalists left the Unitarian churches, schism was ultimately avoided and Unitarians of the present look back upon both parties to the debate as predecessors. The lasting importance of the Transcendentalist controversy lies in the clarity with which two sides of a major philosophical problem were presented. The controversy was no "tempest in a Boston teacup" (as it has been condescendingly termed),[26] but one of the memorable debates in the history of religious thought.

Transcendentalism was not a "mass" movement, but it made up in quality what it lacked in quantity. The Transcendentalists include some of the greatest names in American literary and intellectual history: Ralph Waldo Emerson, Henry David Thoreau, Theodore Parker, George Bancroft, and Margaret Fuller among them. All the Transcendentalists except James Marsh of Vermont emerged from a Unitarian context. Of the twenty-six members of the "Transcendental Club" (the closest thing to comprehensive institutionalization this highly individualistic group achieved), seventeen were Unitarian ministers.[27] The principal—though not the only—center of the "New School" was Concord, Massachusetts. How the Transcendentalists viewed their cause is best described by Emerson: "There are always two parties, the party of the Past and the party of the Future; the Establishment and the Movement." The Transcendentalists considered themselves "the Movement" of the 1830s, invoking what they called "a new consciousness."[28] To a number of bright young people educated since

Channing's Baltimore Sermon of 1819, that formulation of Unitarianism no longer seemed liberal enough. While they always honored Channing's own open-mindedness, the Transcendentalists worried lest his views settle into a new Unitarian orthodoxy in the hands of his successors.

Defining the beliefs common to the Transcendentalists that distinguished them from more conservative (or less radical) Unitarians is difficult. Such a definition is precisely the sort of enterprise the Transcendentalists deplored, for they hated codifications. Indeed, their desire to "transcend" just this kind of thinking gave them their name. The Transcendentalists were essentially pantheists, people who saw and felt God everywhere—in all creation and especially in themselves. They read considerably in Hindu mysticism, which attracted them because of its insistence on the immanence of divinity in the universe. Material things they were inclined to treat as symbols of divine things. Christopher Cranch, Unitarian-minister-turned-Transcendental-poet, wrote: "Every object that speaks to the senses was meant for the spirit. Nature is but a scroll, God's hand-writing thereon." [29] Even more than Oriental seers, European romantics like Goethe, Coleridge, and Carlyle stimulated American Transcendentalism. The Transcendentalists admired not only the romantics' love of nature but also their glorification of passion. Ever since the time of Chauncy, New England religious liberals had insisted that the emotions ought to be guided by the intellect; now Emerson complained this had left the standard Unitarianism of his day "corpse-cold." [30] Emerson had a gift for pithy remarks, and his characterization, while not altogether accurate, has haunted Unitarians ever since.

In many ways Transcendentalism was a logical outgrowth of Unitarianism. An insistence upon human freedom and dignity that had been maintained against Calvinism led quite naturally to an exultation in spontaneity and self-expression. The Unitarian emphasis on literature rather than on dogmatic theology as a medium for expressing religious concerns obviously prepared the way for the amazing "flowering" of Transcendental writings that suddenly burst forth in 1836 and the years following. The liberals' jealously guarded right of private judgment in matters religious culminated in Transcendental faith in personal communion with the divine spirit. Yet for all the continuities between Transcendentalism and the Unitarianism that preceded it, the differences were also real. There is a distinction between rejoicing in mankind's "likeness to God," as Channing did, and declaring, as Emerson did, "I am part or parcel of God." [31]

We may recognize in the Transcendentalist controversy something of a generational conflict, in which those who had won the struggles of liberalism in their day found themselves suddenly confronted by sons and daughters for whom this liberalism was inadequate and outmoded. The Transcendentalists disparaged not only the religion of conventional Unitarians but also their lifestyle. The bourgeois, commercial values of cities like Boston and New York seemed tame and restrictive to them. One profound interpreter of the Transcendentalist controversy (the late Perry Miller) proposed that the "New School" could actually be viewed as a rebirth of old-time Puritan piety and zeal, struggling against the bonds of a Unitarianism grown stale and complacent.[32] It is probably true that some youthful intellectuals of New England in the 1830s were rediscovering an emotional immediacy in their religious experience comparable to that of the Puritan Reformers or of evangelicals like Jonathan Edwards. For this reason, the appearance of Transcendentalism is appropriately conceived as a religious awakening, or a movement for "church reform." [33]

Although there had been earlier rumblings, the opening shot in the Transcendentalist controversy was fired by Emerson in an address to the graduating class at Harvard Divinity School, July 15, 1838. Emerson, himself once a student at the Divinity School, had served as assistant to Henry Ware, Jr., in the Second Church in Boston and then succeeded him when Ware left to become a professor at Harvard. Emerson came to feel even the minimal ritual of Unitarian services irksome, and he particularly objected to the Lord's Supper as an obsolete formality. "Most men find the bread and wine no aid to devotion, and to some it is a painful impediment." [34] Rather than continue to administer the rite, he had resigned in 1832. However, he continued to preach for several years on a substitute basis in neighboring parishes and was still addressed as "reverend" when the Divinity School invited him to speak. Emerson took advantage of the forum thus offered to give vent to frustrations that had long been building up inside him.

Probably he was reacting against the dull sermons of the minister in Concord to whom he had had to listen recently, and, on a deeper level, against his father, the deceased William Emerson, minister of the First Church in Boston, whom the son had always undervalued.[35] But Emerson's audience was interested in the substance of his views, not in accounting for them psychologically.

Organized religion had degenerated into the custodian of a dead faith, Emerson charged, and he did not exempt Unitarianism from the indictment. Unitarianism was still relying upon the supernatural rationalism that had been a prominent feature of eighteenth-century liberal religion, the doctrine that Christ's teachings had been authenticated by the miracles he performed. For Emerson this supernatural rationalism was a grotesque distortion of religion. "To aim to convert a man by miracles is a profanation of the soul. A true conversion, a true Christ, is now, as always, to be made by the reception of beautiful sentiments." [36] What the times needed was the spirit of poetic intuition that would give people direct access to the divine instead of the "second-hand" religion taught in the churches. God was perceived in the beauty of nature around us and in the moral law within ourselves. Defying the importance most Unitarians then accorded to Christian revelation, Emerson declared that scripture and accounts of ancient miracles were irrelevant. Instead of a historic faith in Christ, Emerson called upon his hearers to espouse a "faith like Christ's in the infinitude of man." Commune with nature and "dare to love God without mediator or veil," he urged.[37]

While some younger listeners rejoiced in what Emerson had to say, most of their teachers were appalled. They felt Emerson had betrayed the spirit of the occasion by criticizing the basic premises of traditional Unitarianism within the very citadel of Unitarian theology. After the students returned in September, Henry Ware, Jr., wasted no time in delivering a sermon to them entitled "The Personality of the Deity." While not mentioning Emerson by name, Ware was unmistakably referring to the latter's recent address when he declared that God must not be equated with the universe he had created, nor with abstractions like "beauty" and "virtue." Either God was a personality who took a personal interest in each of us, or else the whole of religion was a waste of time. Emerson's position, divested of its lyrical rhetoric, came down to atheism, Ware concluded.[38] Since the two men had been friends and colleagues for so long, Ware privately invited Emerson to issue a rebuttal or clarification, but Emerson demurred.[39] He was in the process of making a new career as lecturer and poet, moving away from the ministry and denominational affairs. From then on the controversy would be carried on by others.

The two most active critics of Emersonianism were Francis Bowen and Andrews Norton. Scholars of formidable intellect and indefatigable energy, they were not inclined to pull punches in debate. Bowen was a universally learned man, but his principal distinctions lay in economics and philosophy. His contribution to the Transcendentalist controversy took the form of a series of articles in the *Christian Examiner* and the *North American Review*.[40] Together, they constituted a thorough and lucid exposition of traditional theism, placed in a broad context of the history of philosophy. Bowen concluded that the Transcendentalists were giving the appearance of Christianity to views that were in actuality either mere nature-worship or tautologies devoid of content.

While Bowen was rejecting Emersonian pantheism, Andrews Norton assaulted the other half of Transcendentalism, the substitution of personal inspiration for revelation contained in the Bible. In 1838 Norton had published the first volume of his *Evidences of the Genuineness of the Gospels*. This ambitious work employed the recent methods of "higher criticism" developed in Germany to justify the four gospels as authentic. Massive as it was, the study was dismissed by its Transcendentalist reviewer, Orestes Brownson, as dealing with "a matter of comparative indifference." Transcendentalists "have in themselves a witness for God," and do not require either scripture or scriptural scholarship to confirm it.[41] Norton's answer to this contention was delivered in an address to the alumni of Harvard Divinity School on July 19, 1839.

"The latest form of infidelity is distinguished by assuming the Christian name, while it strikes directly at the root of faith in Christianity, and indirectly of all religion, by denying the miracles attesting the divine mission of Christ," he told his audience.[42] The term "infidelity" implied that the "New School" was but

Ralph Waldo Emerson

Joseph Tuckerman

Horace Mann

Theodore Parker

another version of eighteenth-century deism, the denial of revealed religion. The miracles were essential to Norton because if
they had really occurred, they provided solid evidence that Jesus
Christ was what he claimed to be: the Son of God, a divinely appointed messenger whose teachings were true. It was not enough
to look within one's own heart, or at the wonders of nature, to
find religion; too many dangers of wishful thinking lay that way.
"Religious principle and feeling, however important," Norton insisted, "are necessarily founded on the belief of certain facts." [43]
A true liberal in religion relied upon evidence for his convictions.
What better evidence of special divine interposition could there
be than the raising of the dead or the performance of other nor-
mally impossible feats?

The merit in Norton's position may not be easy to recognize
today, because the "evidence" he invoked is no longer credible to
most. But taken as a defense of empirical inquiry, his argument is
admirable. Rational evidence should be the basis for belief or
disbelief in any proposition, he was saying, and religious proposi-
tions are no different from others. To make up our minds on any
issue—in this case the truth of Christianity—we must examine
the evidence. Behind this assertion lay the full weight of Lockean
philosophy, natural science, and the Enlightenment. Norton's research confirmed for him that the facts bore out the miracles, and
the miracles bore out Unitarian Christianity. But this conclusion
was less significant philosophically than his statement: "there is,
then, no mode of establishing religious belief, but by the exercise
of reason, by investigation." [44]

The Transcendentalist party was not without its own learned
expositors. Their response came quickly, in a pamphlet by George
Ripley, minister of the Church in Purchase Street, Boston.[45] A
former student of Norton's, Ripley was almost as erudite (and
almost as forbidding) as he.[46] Ripley did not dispute whether
Christ had walked on water, healed the sick, or come back from
the dead; he was willing to affirm that these miracles occurred.
Instead, Ripley attacked the philosophical foundation of Norton's
position. Ripley maintained that one did not arrive at religious
conviction by evaluating evidence. Instead, one made what would
later be called an initial "leap of faith," an inner response to the
call of a divine power outside. Ripley did not mean that religious

knowledge was not real, substantive knowledge, but that it was apprehended through a different faculty than was mundane data. Transcendentalists believed human powers of cognition included not only the "understanding," through which secular information was assimilated, but also what they called the "reason," by which they meant an intuitive power to discern divine things. Norton's process of weighing evidence applied only to things of the "understanding," they claimed. If Norton's argument was that of the Enlightenment, Ripley's reply was that of the Romantic era.

Ripley's perspective on religion had its advantages, though in the eyes of Norton it was irresponsible "mystagogy." [47] The trouble with relying upon miracles as evidence for religion is that few people credit miracles unless they first accept religion. People believe in the Christian miracles because they believe in the Gospels, Ripley observed, not the other way around. Faith, then, has priority in religion. Norton and Ripley each issued three long statements in the course of their debate, for they canvassed contemporary European writings to illustrate their points. The true nature of religion will perhaps always remain a subject of controversy, but some of the fundamental issues have never been drawn with greater precision on both sides than in this confrontation.[48]

IV

Before the Transcendentalist controversy was over, it had become almost as bitter and personal as the Unitarian-Calvinist controversy that preceded it. The conservative Unitarians accused the "New School" of hiding dangerously anarchic and blasphemous implications in cryptic utterances—much as the orthodox had accused the early religious liberals of doing. The Transcendentalists accused their adversaries of snobbery. It was undemocratic to rely upon historical accounts, such as the miracle stories, for authentication of religion, they complained, because only a few scholars had the expertise necessary to evaluate such evidence. The egalitarian spirit of the age and the needs of ordinary churchmen required that religion be placed on a basis which all could know first-hand: the promptings of their own souls.[49] To this the answer was that if religion contains a body of knowledge like other knowledge, there ought to be nothing objectionable in the existence of trained experts in it.[50] Indeed, conventional Unitarian opinion had always maintained the necessity for proper training in morality as well as religion. In a significant private exchange, Channing told Theodore Parker the conscience needed educating, but the Transcendentalist minister objected, calling the moral faculty "infallible" in all people.[51]

It was Parker who provoked the next stage in the controversy. Despite his disparagement of the moral usefulness of education, Parker was a man of vast learning and still vaster energies. The eleventh child of a poor farmer, he had learned twenty languages and assimilated German "higher criticism" at first hand. He ministered to the Unitarian church in West Roxbury, then a small rural community. When the Hawes Place Church in South Boston invited him to preach for the ordination of their new minister (Charles C. Shackford) on May 19, 1841, Parker startled everyone by turning his sermon into a general proclamation of Transcendentalist principles. He entitled it "The Transient and Permanent in Christianity."

The essence of Christianity is of "permanent" validity, Parker declared, but many aspects of the religion are merely "transient," varying from age to age. Liberals had long employed such a doctrine of "progressive revelation" to explain passages in the Old Testament that seemed ethically primitive.[52] But when Parker came to identify that which was transient in religion, he did not stop with early Jewish misapprehensions; he included all "creeds, confessions, and collections of doctrines." [53] More bothersome, Parker placed all the scriptures in the "transient" category. He pointed out that the biblical criticism Unitarians like Norton were promoting would inevitably undercut the authority of the New as well as the Old Testament, making both look less like timeless oracles and more like historical texts of limited applicability to the present. Most disturbing of all, Parker denied "permanent" status to the personal authority of Christ. He went so far as to declare that if "Jesus of Nazareth had never lived, still Christianity would stand firm." [54]

What was the Christianity that could exist independently of Christ? For Parker it was pure morality, as known to the individual conscience, or what Transcendentalists termed "Reason." Parker's sermon is at once iconoclastic and humble. "No doubt an age will come in which ours shall be reckoned a period of darkness—like the sixth century—when men groped for the wall but stumbled and fell, because they trusted a transient notion, not an eternal truth." [55] His doctrine is the ultimate logic of religious individualism. In place of the infallible church of the Catholics and the infallible book of the Protestants, the "New School" had put an infallible private power of spiritual perception.

Parker's sermon had been attended by three Trinitarian clergymen. Appalled by what they had heard, these ministers demanded to know whether such radical opinions were generally approved by Unitarians. This forced the Unitarian community to take the unprecedented step of considering whether there were any doctrinal limitations to their fellowship. The Transcendentalists were a small minority among Unitarians, and the majority did not want to be misunderstood as favoring "Parkerism." No mechanism existed for heresy trials or excommunication, but there were ways in which Parker's views could be disowned by others. The Boston Association of Ministers, a Unitarian group of which Parker was a member, discussed his ideas with him and asked him to resign. To their discomfiture, he refused to do so. Parker's colleagues were unwilling to abandon their commitment to free inquiry to the extent of formally expelling him; however, they left his name off their published roster of members. Most of the clergy in the area stopped exchanging pulpits with Parker, and when John T. Sargent of the ministry-at-large exchanged with him in 1844, the Benevolent Fraternity of Churches reprimanded him. Sargent then resigned. [56]

There seemed no end to the ways in which Parker could embarrass his fellow Unitarians. An "ecclesiastical council" of local ministers had tried to arbitrate a dispute between an outspoken reforming minister, John Pierpont, and his offended Hollis Street congregation by recommending against dismissal, while also reproaching the pastor for his conduct. Parker, incensed at such equivocation, called the council's report "a piece of diplomacy worthy of a college of Jesuits." [57] Then, in December 1844, Parker took his turn at delivering the "Great and Thursday Lecture" traditionally preached by the Congregational (now, of course, Unitarian) ministers of the Boston area in rotation. He spoke on "The

Relation of Jesus to His Age and the Ages." Jesus was the greatest
person who has ever lived, Parker acknowledged, but he may
have taught some errors along with his truths, and Parker expected that "God has yet greater men in store." [58] Unlike Ripley,
Parker denied the historicity of Christ's miracles. The Boston
Association of Ministers was horrified; when Parker refused to
give up his right to preach again, members returned control of
the lectureship to the First Church of Boston, whence it had
originated centuries before. Without Parker's participation the
lectures could not sustain public interest, so after a few years the
First Church discontinued the series.[59] Official Unitarianism preferred to end one of New England's most distinguished religious
traditions rather than permit it to be used by Parker.

But the embattled Transcendentalist did not lack a following.
In 1845 a group of sympathetic laymen in Boston organized the
Twenty-Eighth Congregational Society and invited Parker to become their minister. The Twenty-Eighth was more a lecture forum
than a conventional church; Parker preached in the Melodeon
Theater until 1852 and thereafter in the Music Hall. Accommodating the crowds, which sometimes reached three thousand,
was always a problem. None of the other Boston clergymen could
regularly command such audiences; no doubt this added to their
resentment. Parker posed a more difficult problem for the clerical
conservatives than Emerson (or Ripley, who resigned his pastorate
in 1841) because he would not leave the ministry. Refusal to exchange pulpits was a weapon the orthodox had earlier used against
liberals, and Parker reminded the Boston Association of Ministers
that "some of you are pursuing the same course you once complained of." [60] Yet they persisted in their course. "No principle of
liberality or charity can require any one to aid in the diffusion of
what he accounts error, especially if he thinks it pernicious error,"
Ezra Stiles Gannett correctly observed.[61] To acknowledge the conservatives' right to oppose Parker should not, of course, detract
from the recognition of his courage in the face of their opposition.

At the time the American Unitarian Association had been
formed, religious liberals had taken for granted a dual commitment to freedom of inquiry and Christian revelation. But in 1853,
annoyed that Parker's Transcendental ideas were continuing to
attract some younger ministers, the Executive Committee of the

A.U.A. issued a "declaration of opinion" emphasizing revelation at the expense of freedom. "The divine authority of the Gospel, as founded on a special and miraculous interposition of God for the redemption of mankind, is the basis of the action of this Association," it read. The declaration blamed the slow growth of Unitarianism on the Transcendentalists and the "odium" they were bringing upon liberals.[62] While there was no way to enforce conformity to its precepts, this statement must stand as the closest American Unitarians have ever come to creed-making. Though the Unitarian denomination has honored him since his death, in his lifetime Parker and his views were repudiated by organized Unitarianism. As he lay dying in Italy in 1859-60, prematurely exhausted from his labors, the alumni of the Harvard Divinity School refused to adopt a resolution of sympathy for him.[63]

Transcendentalist efforts to put their principles into practice sometimes compounded their difficulties with other Unitarians. The Transcendentalists applied their principles in two different, one might say opposite, directions. One route lay in perfecting the individual, drawing out his authentic self and placing him in harmony with nature. The other lay in perfecting society at large, so as to make it more conducive to the self-realization of its members. Several notable Transcendentalists conducted experiments of the first sort. Bronson Alcott's Temple School, founded in Boston in 1834, pioneered what would later be called progressive education. If spiritual awareness was intuitive and innate, as Transcendentalists insisted, it must be manifested in children. Accordingly, there was no corporal punishment at Temple School, and children were encouraged to express themselves, even on controversial subjects. After only three years, Alcott's school collapsed when parents discovered he was mentioning (in ways that seem mild and abstract today) sex in the classroom.[64] Other Transcendental enterprises included communities that attempted to develop alternative life-styles where the individual could commune with God through nature. The most famous of these was Brook Farm in West Roxbury, organized by Ripley just before he left his parish. Many intellectuals of the day spent varying periods in this little utopia, immortalized by Nathaniel Hawthorne's novel *The Blithedale Romance*. In 1844 Brook Farm adopted a socialistic plan devised by the Frenchman Charles Fourier, but the commune came to an end in 1847 after a fire had destroyed some of its newest facilities.[65] The greatest of all Transcendental experiments in perfecting the individual, however, was the one-man utopia of Henry David Thoreau at Walden Pond outside Concord.

Transcendental efforts to remake society were regarded at the time as radical. Orestes Brownson, an eccentric and impetuous man ordained successively to the Universalist and Unitarian ministries, founded the *Boston Quarterly Review* in 1838. Through this organ he proclaimed Transcendental religious principles combined with working-class political agitation until 1844, when he suddenly abandoned both for proslavery conservatism and the Roman Catholic Church.[66] A more persistent radical was Margaret Fuller, editor of *The Dial* from 1840 to 1844. This Transcendentalist periodical had a circulation of three hundred or less, and contemporaries dismissed it as representing a lunatic fringe; today it is more highly regarded than any other American magazine of its era. A child prodigy who became in adulthood one of America's leading feminists, Margaret Fuller was accepted only in the most avant-garde circles. (The Transcendental Club included five women.) She was generally regarded as aggressive—a trait considered ludicrously inappropriate in a woman. Her most influential book, *Woman in the Nineteenth Century* (1845), manifested her quest for a more positive feminine identity. While in Italy reporting on the revolution of Mazzini, she fell in love with young Giovanni Ossoli and bore him a child before their marriage, scandalizing her countrymen. In 1850 all three Ossolis were drowned in a shipwreck.[67]

Having cast aside most institutions and conventions, the Transcendentalists were more unreservedly antislavery than most other Unitarians. Parker was in the forefront of militant abolitionism, a confidant of Sumner and other antislavery politicians. It is more than coincidental that Ezra Stiles Gannett, one of the most conservative Unitarian ministers on the slavery issue, took a major part in mobilizing opposition to Parker's theology. Transcendentalists placed moral intuition above written law, as they placed religious intuition above written scripture. Parker helped fugitive slaves to freedom and conspired with John Brown regarding his raid. Unlike William Lloyd Garrison (who joined his Twenty-Eighth Congregational Society), Parker felt no scruples about employing violence in a just cause. Among those associated with Parker in civil disobedience was Thomas Wentworth Higginson. After a ministry to the First Religious Society of Newburyport (1847-50), this Transcendental activist found a congregation more in tune with his religious and political views at the Free Church in Worcester, Massachusetts (1852-58). There he openly boasted of harboring fugitive slaves: "Let the Underground Railroad stop here!" he cried. "Henceforth Worcester is Canada to the slave!" [68] Higginson and Parker played prominent roles in the unsuccessful attempt to rescue Anthony Burns, but the ensuing prosecution of them was unsuccessful. During the Civil War Higginson became celebrated as one of the white officers who commanded black troops in the Union army. Both Parker and Higginson combined their abolitionism with resolute support for the cause of women's rights.

The spectacle of Unitarians bitterly disagreeing with each other during the Transcendentalist controversy gave aid and comfort to orthodox churchmen who had never wished the liberal community well. This, plus the strong ties of fellowship and consanguinity among Unitarians, explains why a significant number of clergymen sought to mediate between the two sides to the controversy. Channing managed to stay on good personal terms with most of the Transcendentalists until his death in 1842, though his firm adherence to the views of Norton and Ware keenly disappointed them. James Walker, editor of the *Christian Examiner* and later president of Harvard, tried to play a conciliatory role, as did Convers Francis, professor in the Divinity School. Among the most noteworthy of the moderates was Frederic Henry Hedge, pastor of churches in Bangor, Maine (1835-50), and Providence, Rhode Island (1850-56). A deeply learned and sensitive man, his concerns went beyond mere ecclesiastical faction-balancing. He forged a Unitarian theology that blended traditional Protestant and contemporary Transcendental elements in ways analogous to the Christian romanticism of Coleridge.[69] The strength of his faith is indicated in his familiar translation of Luther's hymn, "A Mighty Fortress is Our God."

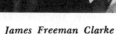

James Freeman Clarke   *Thomas Starr King*

In the long run Transcendentalism, or at least the memory of
it, was destined to be reabsorbed within Unitarianism. This
rapprochement owes more to James Freeman Clarke than to any
other single person. Clarke had been reared by his father's step-
father, James Freeman of King's Chapel; he was also a distant
cousin and close platonic friend of Margaret Fuller. These relationships illustrate the intimacy he preserved with both traditional and Transcendental Unitarians all his life. During the
1830s Clarke headed a new Unitarian church in Louisville, Kentucky, edited a Transcendental magazine called the *Western
Messenger*, and supported Ripley in the debate with Norton. In
1841 he established the Church of the Disciples in Boston, which
served as an example of possible reconciliation between Transcendentalism and something like conventional Unitarian parish
life. Like Hedge, Clarke found the terminology of traditional
Christianity a congenial mode of expression. Though he exchanged with Parker and was energetically antislavery, Clarke
served on the Executive Committee of the A.U.A., becoming its
secretary in 1859.[70]

V

As Clarke's service in Kentucky attests, there were occasional
efforts throughout the middle third of the nineteenth century to

turn Unitarianism into a truly national, rather than local, movement. Unitarian churches began to appear outside New England as colonies of migrating New Englanders undertook to maintain familiar ties. The Unitarians of New York City, who included such prominent figures as Bryant, Dewey, the merchant-philanthropist Moses Grinnell, and Henry W. Bellows, minister of the First Church (after 1855 called All Souls), became especially important in broadening the geographical perspectives of the liberal community.[71] Unitarianism also extended into upstate New York: President Fillmore and his wife belonged to the congregation in Buffalo; Samuel J. May combined a conventional Unitarian pastorate at Syracuse with some of the most effective abolitionist and women's rights agitation conducted anywhere. The growth of Unitarianism in the southern states, however, was inhibited by its antislavery tendencies and general reputation for innovation. Despite the faithful labors of Samuel Gilman in Charleston, South Carolina, Unitarianism endured but a precarious existence in a few commercial centers below the Mason-Dixon line.[72]

Wherever Unitarian churches sprang up, they generally served a constituency that was urban, prosperous, and well educated. It inevitably took a while before such constituencies appeared on the western frontier, and Harvard Divinity School graduates were often reluctant to leave familiar surroundings to take up ministries there. For some years most of the effort to propagate liberal religion in the trans-Allegheny West was undertaken not by Unitarians but by two other small denominations, the Universalists and the Christian Connection. But in 1844 Unitarians established a theological seminary at Meadville, Pennsylvania, under the patronage of James Freeman Clarke's father-in-law, a wealthy Dutch-American immigrant named Harm Jan Huidekoper. From the beginning Meadville graduates took an interest in missionary work, and a Western Unitarian Conference was organized in 1852. The same year the Christian Connection founded Antioch College in Yellow Springs, Ohio. Horace Mann became its first president, and in 1865 the young college was turned over to the Unitarians.

The greatest of Unitarian emissaries in the West was Thomas Starr King. Originally a Universalist clergyman, he accepted a call from the Hollis Street Unitarian Church, Boston, in 1848.

King had a reputation for wit; he apparently originated the oft-repeated distinction between Universalists and Unitarians: "the one thinks God is too good to damn them forever, the other thinks they are too good to be damned forever." [73] A successful lecturer as well as preacher, King was second only to Parker as a popular pulpit orator. He enjoyed good relations with both conservative and Transcendental Unitarians. In 1860 King left New England to lead the new Unitarian congregation in San Francisco. There he played an important role in binding California to the cause of the Union during the crucial opening months of the Civil War and in promoting the work of the Sanitary Commission (the medical supply agency for the northern army).

The Civil War proved an important turning point in Unitarian history. Transcendentalist haters of slavery like Higginson and conservative Union-lovers like Dewey found themselves together supporting the new Republican party and the northern war effort. At James Freeman Clarke's suggestion, the author and feminist Julia Ward Howe (wife of Samuel) wrote "The Battle Hymn of the Republic." [74] Out of the stirring experiences of the war came increased appreciation for the virtues of discipline and unity. Henry W. Bellows of New York, long a convinced believer in what he called "the doctrine of institutions," [75] took advantage of this mood to press for stronger organizational ties among Unitarians. His efforts came to fruition in 1865, when the National Conference of Unitarian Churches was established, and Unitarianism in the United States took on structured denominational form for the first time.

With this development a new chapter in the history of Unitarianism began. Unitarians of the era before 1865 had placed their trust not in such a national institution but primarily in the force of their ideas and example. They lavished their considerable organizational talents upon philanthropic and cultural enterprises, but not upon their sect. "Our object is not to convert men to our party, but to our principles," they had declared.[76] Emphasis upon matters of principle had led Unitarians into social, philosophical, and political controversy; it had even produced internal strife among them. Perhaps men like Bellows were right in feeling that preoccupation with ideology and its implementation had hampered denominational expansion. But if the Unitarians of the middle third of the nineteenth century had neglected ecclesiastical empire-building, they had contributed enormously where they had made their efforts: in the realm of social, literary, and religious ideas.

Meadville Theological School when it was in Meadville, Pennsylvania

Chapter 3

"Salute the Arriving Moment"

Denominational Growth and

the Quest for Consensus, 1865-1895

I

The ending of the Civil War allowed Unitarians to turn their attention afresh to denominational problems. Foremost among them was the loss of momentum that had discouraged many Unitarians in the fifties. In 1859, the prevailing "suspense of faith," as Henry W. Bellows termed it, both in Protestantism at large and the Unitarian body in particular, had been the subject of a widely discussed address he delivered before the alumni of the Harvard Divinity School.[1] Parkerism had meant controversy; as a consequence, some Unitarians had moved back into more orthodox denominations, internal dissent had blunted enthusiasm, financial support for the A.U.A. had fallen off, and few new churches were gathered. It was time for a fresh assessment of the denomination and its prospects.

During the war, while serving as head of the United States Sanitary Commission, Bellows had become convinced that, in the vast social transformation the country was experiencing, the opportunity existed for liberal Christianity to supplant evangelical Protestantism as the dominant religious force in the new nation. But there was no assurance that Unitarianism would be the beneficiary. Unless Unitarians were willing to organize more effectively and on a national basis, he argued, their body would be passed by in the rush of events, fated to "dwindle and die of dignified decency in the narrow track where it has hitherto walked," [2] while religious liberalism found other channels in which to flow. That Unitarianism did not wholly fail to meet the challenge of the day may be attributed in no small measure to Bellows's leadership.

Late in 1864, at a meeting called to consider the financial predicament of the A.U.A., Bellows argued that the crux of the problem was "the want of the proper machinery" for enlisting widespread support from all the churches. Without it, the A.U.A. would be unable to carry on the work of church extension on a scale appropriate to the times. He urged that a convention be called, in which the churches would be represented by delegates, "to consider the interests of our cause and to institute measures for its good." His proposal was unanimously accepted, and he was named chairman of a committee on arrangements. Edward Everett Hale was also on the committee, and he became Bellows's most effective collaborator. [3]

The convention met in New York, April 4-6, 1865, with representatives present from more than three quarters of the churches. [4] It voted to establish a permanent National Conference of Unitarian Churches, to supplement and support the work of the A.U.A. Although the convention did not follow Bellows's lead in every respect, he was the dominating figure in it. He considered it to have been *"an absolute & entire success,"* [5] and the response of Unitarians generally to its work was overwhelmingly favorable.

In the convention, to be sure, the old tensions between conservative Unitarians and the Parkerites or "Radicals" reappeared. The basic disagreement proved to be over the question of how inclusive the new organization should be, and the issue focussed on the name to be adopted. Bellows had been urging for several months that it should be: The Liberal Church of America; his desire was to draw together liberals from many denominations who were drifting away from the evangelical churches. Radicals like Octavius Brooks Frothingham and Francis Ellingwood Abbot were interested to see if the line would be drawn so as to include free spirits who might not even want to call themselves Christians. But the convention proved to be more denominationally minded than Bellows had expected. While it defeated an attempt to tie the organization to a very conservative Christian statement of faith, it described it as a conference of "Christian churches of the Unitarian faith," and put the adjective "Unitarian" in the title. Bellows and Hale accepted the denominational name as a political necessity, given the temper of the convention; what was important, Hale said, was that the Unitarians had demonstrated that they "were a singularly practical body; determined to have some organization, equally determined to have no creed." [6]

The Radicals were less pleased. Abbot was "saddened and disappointed" by the outcome, but argued that the "principles which practically guided the action" of the convention had been better than the sectarian name and conservative preamble that had been adopted. Nevertheless, he declared that he was "full of hope, and not one whit discouraged by the purely embryonic results of our first great conference." [7] A more discordant voice was that of Octavius Brooks Frothingham. He had gone to the convention reluctantly, predisposed to find fault, and was bitterly critical of the result. The convention, he complained, "held to its old sectarian name with a tenacity never before exhibited"; there had never been a convention "so narrow and blind and stubborn as it was." [8]

The denominational structure resulting from the New York convention was a curious hybrid. Already in existence was the American Unitarian Association, founded in 1825 for the purpose of promoting the spread of liberal Christianity by the distribution of tracts and the support of missionary activity. Other denominational functions had gravitated to the desk of its secretary, particularly the supply of vacant pulpits and the placement of ministers. But the A.U.A. was an association of individuals, not a delegate body of the churches. Some Unitarians disapproved of associated activity on principle; others simply ignored it; and the authority of the A.U.A. to speak for the whole Unitarian body was open to question. Furthermore, Bellows felt that, however faithfully the A.U.A. had carried out its mission, it was too much a clerical operation, and in its outlook too much restricted by Boston parochialism. But instead of trying to replace it, or reshape it, Bellows sought to undergird it with a new organization that would supply precisely those elements the A.U.A. lacked.

Hence the National Conference was structured as a representative assembly, in which each church was entitled to one ministerial and two lay delegates. It was to meet annually in various parts of the country (though biennial sessions were soon substituted for annual ones), to hear reports on various aspects of denominational life and work, to listen to speakers on doctrinal and practical issues, to stimulate financial support for denominational causes, and to speak for the denomination as a whole in defining common objectives and policy. The by-laws provided for a council to plan the meetings, and to that end to be in touch with the various organizations in the Unitarian body; and the council was authorized to issue, after each conference, an address to the churches and other organizations "containing such advice and encouragement as it may deem appropriate." But it had no administrative arm of its own to implement policy. Its role was purely advisory, and it adopted the already existing Unitarian organizations, particularly the A.U.A., as the "instruments of its power." [9]

At the second meeting of the National Conference, in 1866, the report of the council, read by Dr. Bellows, argued for a structure of local conferences as well. The invigoration of church life Bellows sought could not be achieved with only an annual or biennial meeting which, because of distance and expense, many delegates would have difficulty in attending. The report advocated that the Unitarian denomination be subdivided territorially, and that each church be a member of a local association or conference. These conferences, predominantly lay, would meet quarterly or oftener, "for fellowship, consultation and the framing of methods and plans for meeting the religious wants of their own allotted sphere, and for co-operation with the general missionary operations of the denomination at large." [10] Indeed, the day might come when the National Conference as originally established would become unwieldy, and would have to be made up of delegates from local conferences, rather than directly from the churches.

This proposal was approved by the Conference, and detailed recommendations were prepared by the council and sent to the churches. By the time the National Conference next met, in 1870, twenty such local conferences had been formed. While some were as yet no more than paper organizations, others were able to report well-attended meetings, more effective fund-raising, new churches established, and generally heightened morale.[11]

A further step in restructuring denominational machinery came in 1884, when the by-laws of the A.U.A. were rewritten to admit delegates from the churches, with voting rights, to meetings of the Association. Individual memberships were not discontinued, but the crucial first step was taken toward making the A.U.A. directly responsible to the churches, and thereby legitimatizing its role in denominational policy-making and implementation.[12] As the annual meetings of the A.U.A. became increasingly the forum in which denominational policy was decided, the biennial sessions of the National Conference were more and more devoted to addresses dealing generally with current theological and social issues.

Evidence of new vitality in the denomination is unmistakable in the reports of the A.U.A. and the National Conference, and in denominational journals. Annual giving for the general purposes of the Association, even allowing for inflationary times, made a quantum jump. In 1863, the total was a meager $3,056; in 1864, it was $6,409. In 1865, a special drive, to which the New York convention gave impetus, produced more than $100,000. In 1867, the amount raised was $54,827, and the following year, $42,687.[13] Giving to special projects also increased: $100,000 was raised in 1865 for Antioch College, then under Unitarian auspices. For the first time in a generation, missionary efforts began to achieve substantial success. In 1850, there were 251 churches listed in the yearbook, and fifteen years later, only 259. But in the decade from 1865 to 1875, the number rose to 349.[14] The denomination was still a small one; the major breakthrough of which Bellows had dreamed had not been achieved. But the movement was upward; the stagnation of the fifties was over.

From 1865 until his death in 1882, Henry W. Bellows was the leading spirit of organized or denominational Unitarianism. Collaborators he had, to be sure: men like Edward Everett Hale and James Freeman Clarke, who had worked with him in founding the National Conference, and Charles Lowe, secretary of the A.U.A. But he was the one who drew the energies of the denomination into harness. No one in the denomination had a wider range of contacts than he; none was more fertile in conceiving new projects to advance the common cause or more eager in persuading Unitarians to support them; none was more effective in speaking before public meetings or readier to devote whatever time was needed to committee work. His own generation heard him willingly, followed him gladly, and freely acknowledged indebtedness to him. There is a very special sense, wrote Joseph Henry Allen, "in which the period [after 1865], with the wider scale and greater variety of denominational activity, is best represented by the name of Dr. Bellows."[15] He was "our Bishop, our Metropolitan," said Frederic Henry Hedge. "The dignity is unknown by name in our communion. . . . But this once in our history, by this one man in our brotherhood, the function was exercised, and that by no robbery but by universal consent of the brethren." [16] John White Chadwick, whose theological position was very different from that of Bellows, and who was usually regarded as a Radical, declared that "almost every best thing that has been devised for the last seventeen years within the limits of the Unitarian denomination has taken its initiative from him or to his splendid advocacy owed its practical success." [17] Even Cyrus A. Bartol, for whom organization held no attraction, said quite simply: "Dr. Bellows is the only leader the Unitarian body has ever had." [18]

II

At the New York convention, Bellows sought to create a wide consensus in support of more effective denominational organization. His strategy was to enlarge and strengthen the "broad church" group, as he termed it, which occupied a middle ground between the conservative Unitarians who were ready to disown the Parkerites as non-Christian, and the Radicals who felt that it was a violation of their freedom for the new organization to assume a Christian identity. He was delighted to find that the two wings were weaker, and the main body was stronger, than he had supposed in advance might be the case.

But the two wings were not amputated, and so the issues creating tension within the denomination persisted. If part of the history of the denomination for the next thirty years is the story of enlarged activity, growing denominational consciousness, and increased numerical strength, another part of that history is the struggle for a resolution of internal theological differences and the achievement of a new consensus.

This quest for consensus was carried on at a time of great ferment in all the denominations, confronted as they were by the several intellectual challenges represented by Darwinism, the science of biblical criticism, and the study of comparative religions. The interweaving of intellectual forces in American Unitarianism in this generation was extremely complex, has been inadequately studied, and is imperfectly understood. Any attempt at explication must be regarded as tentative, and subject to revision and refinement.

A plausible starting point for analysis would be a discrimination among several different theological positions within the denomination. Reading from right to left, they may be identified as follows: the Evangelicals; the Older Rationalists; the younger conservatives and the Christian transcendentalists who together made up Bellows's "Broad Church" group; and the "Radicals," some of whom were transcendentalist and intuitional in their philosophy, while others were empirical and scientific. This classification is one that Bellows himself developed, when he was weighing the prospects for success at the New York convention in 1865.[19]

(1) *The Evangelicals.* Unitarianism has often included some who have never been quite sure whether they belonged in the denomination or in one of the more conservative Protestant bodies. Sometimes they were Unitarian in their Christology, but longed for a more evangelical kind of piety or a more liturgical mode of worship. Some of them changed their affiliation; others remained within the fold, though not wholly at ease there. In 1858 and 1860 there were two conspicuous examples of prominent Boston ministers who entered the Episcopal church, J. I. T. Coolidge and Frederic Dan Huntington.[20] In 1869, after twenty years as minister of the Church of the Messiah in New York, Dr. Samuel Osgood followed them; and two years later, his successor, George H. Hepworth, became a Congregationalist. Of those who remained Unitarian, one may cite Rufus Ellis of the First Church in Boston, and Edmund Hamilton Sears of Weston.

This group was characterized by a strong loyalty to Jesus Christ as Lord and Saviour. Sometimes they held higher views of the role of Christ than prevailed generally in the denomination—in the cases of Huntington and Sears, notably so. In any event, Jesus was very much the focus of their religious emotions. They were distressed by the presence within the denomination of radicals who seemed to be losing all sense of the uniqueness of Jesus. In 1865, Bellows asserted that they "want to *secede* & are disposed to deny any fellowship with the looser & more liberal party." [21] They were at best reluctant participants in the New York convention, which Ellis declined to attend, since they were not eager to accentuate a denominational boundary line between Unitarianism and the rest of the Christian community.

(2) *The Older Rationalists.* The Unitarian right wing shaded imperceptibly from the Evangelicals into the Older Rationalists. These represented a continuation of the Unitarianism of the first generation. They were schooled in the writings of the Scottish "common sense" realists, and accepted as axiomatic the prevailing Christian apologetics sometimes called "Supernatural Rationalism" by recent historians.[22] That is to say, for them Christianity was validated, not by inner religious experience, but by the historical evidence of the divine mission of Jesus as attested by miracles. They sometimes described themselves as "Channing Unitarians" by way of contrast with the Transcendentalists, for whom the primary validation of religion itself is the inner consciousness, not historical evidence.

Bellows referred to these as the *"elder men,* old fashioned Unitarians," and identified Ezra Stiles Gannett of the Arlington Street Church as perhaps "the head of this section." [23] They were the conservatives that Bellows had to placate at the New York convention, since they represented a very considerable segment of the denomination. Their position was advanced in a motion presented early in the convention, which would have tied the National Conference to an explicitly Christian doctrinal basis. Its character is well indicated by the following paragraph:

> Belief in our Lord, Jesus Christ, our Saviour, the Son of God and His specially appointed Messenger and Representative to our race; gifted with supernatural power, 'approved of God by miracles and signs and wonders which God did by him,' and thus, by Divine authority, commanding the devout and reverential faith of all who claim the Christian name . . .[24]

Bellows succeeded in sidetracking this resolution, the effect of which would have been to place the Conference on a creedal basis; for while no formal procedures of testing and exclusion were indicated, a standard would have been erected by which Christian Unitarians could have called the Radicals to account and have challenged their participation. And so, while the Evangelicals reacted to the presence of the Radicals by recoiling or withdrawing, these Older Rationalists reacted by seeking to draw a line which would make the Radicals themselves feel excluded.

(3) *The Broad Church Group.* The "Broad Church" group shared the Christian commitment of the Evangelicals and the Older Rationalists, and were not disposed to remake Unitarianism into a movement of free spirits in which Jesus Christ—in Bellows's words—would be put "into comparative contempt." [25] But unlike conservatives of the older type, they did not seek to exclude the Radicals, but rather tried to draw them in. The Broad Church men, Bellows said, "recognize the elements of truth in all the other sections & believe in the possibility of welding them together . . ." [26] Given the Christian loyalties of the great majority of the denomination, some of the Radicals might choose an independent course, but no creedal definitions to promote exclusion would be tolerated. As Bellows put it: "We want to describe a large eno' circle to take in all who really belong with us—and provided one, and the *fixed* leg of the compasses is in the heart of Jesus Christ I care very little how wide & far the other wanders." [27]

To identify the Broad Church group, to which he himself claimed to belong, Bellows pointed to James Freeman Clarke, Edward Everett Hale, and Frederic Henry Hedge. Two of these men—Clarke and Hedge—had early been identified with the Transcendentalists. The other two—Hale and Bellows—quite definitely had not. Yet they all collaborated effectively in 1865 and worked together congenially thereafter. This suggests that there is something seriously askew in the common assumption that the Radicals of 1865, who became the Free Religionists of 1867, were the proper heirs of Emerson and Parker, while the "conservatives" of the New York convention represented a continuation of the "corpse-cold" Unitarianism against which the Transcendentalists had rebelled. That is history seen through Radical eyes. It does not represent the way the lines of cleavage actually were drawn;

for the divisive issues of 1865 and 1866, though not unrelated to the issues disputed in the Transcendentalist controversy, were differently accented and produced a different alignment of forces.

Indeed, the initial distinction between Transcendentalist and non-Transcendentalist proved to be of very fleeting importance. Transcendentalists began by rejecting the empirical philosophy of John Locke, which derived all knowledge from sense impressions. This was the philosophical underpinning of the theology of the Older Rationalists, who emphasized the evidences in the gospels that Jesus Christ was a divinely authorized messenger. For this "heart-withering" philosophy, as Emerson termed it, the Transcendentalists would substitute a philosophy of intuition, declaring that the great truths of religion are given as facts of consciousness, not grounded in historical evidences.

But when Andrews Norton condemned Transcendentalism, his objections to the intuitional philosophy as such were subordinate to his main concern, namely, that it would lead to a rejection of Christianity as a religion authenticated by verifiable historical events. He was right in suggesting that Transcendentalism tended that way; he was wrong if he supposed that an abandonment of the Christian tradition would invariably be the outcome. It soon became apparent—and Hedge is the most striking example—that there would be those who would combine an intuitional epistemology with a sense of the uniqueness or even the finality of the Christian religion, just as Lockean empiricism could produce either Deism (which denied the Christian revelation) or Supernatural Rationalism (which affirmed it). So the real issue that divided Emerson from Norton in 1839, or Parker from his critics in the years that followed, was not epistemology, but the relationship between Christianity and what Parker termed "Absolute Religion." So readily was the question of epistemology submerged that scholars to this day may be found arguing whether, on the basis of an adherence to an intuitional epistemology, Parker was a genuine Transcendentalist or not.[28]

(4) *The Radicals.* These were the free spirits in the denomination who refused to acknowledge for Christianity any special rank among the religious traditions of mankind, on grounds either of its supernatural origin, or its exalted doctrine, or its beneficial consequences. They were marked also by a great concern lest the

integrity of individual belief be compromised by ecclesiasticism. To identify them, Bellows pointed to Octavius Brooks Frothingham, Samuel Longfellow, William J. Potter, "and a strong body of young men just out of Divinity Studies." His characterization of them was brief and perceptive: "transcendental in their philosophy, unhistorical in their faith . . . who really think Xty only one among a great many other Religions, excellent in their way, & in fact doubt if there be not something better *coming*." Even before the New York convention, Bellows was aware of their reluctance to participate, "thinking some test may be applied, some creed slipped round them." [29]

These were the men who complained of the denominational name adopted for the National Conference and saw creedalism in its Preamble. After their unsuccessful attempt to amend the Preamble at Syracuse in 1866, some of them formed the Free Religious Association as a forum for the expression of more advanced religious ideas than Unitarianism seemed ready to accept. The F.R.A. had not been in existence long, however, before internal differences emerged. Emerson had been invited to address its first meeting, and some of the preliminary discussions leading up to its formation had been held in the living room of Dr. Cyrus A. Bartol of the West Church in Boston. These names are a reminder that there was a strong Transcendentalist component in Free Religion. But the F.R.A. also included men like Francis Ellingwood Abbot, who published in 1871 an attack on the "intuitional school" of Free Religion. For the Transcendentalist, he noted, God and Immortality are given as facts of consciousness, and asserted as dogmatically as any doctrine of Christian orthodoxy. But for the "scientific school," which he himself represented, both these doctrines are open questions, awaiting scientific evidence. "Not only must science so enlarge its sphere as to include the problems of God and Immortality . . . but it must approach their solution by . . . the union of induction and deduction, resting on a basis of observed facts and leading to verifiable results." Pursuing this line of argument, Abbot at a later date attempted the construction of a "scientific theism." [30]

There was another internal division within the ranks of Free Religion, between those who still regarded themselves as Christian, though in some radically revised sense, and those who felt they no longer could conscientiously accept the Christian name. Abbot was perhaps the most conspicuous representative of the latter position, since his decision to reject Christianity while minister of the Unitarian church in Dover, New Hampshire, led to extended litigation over the use of funds bequeathed for the support of the Christian ministry.[31] But Frothingham and Potter adopted a similar position at a somewhat later date. Just as, at the conservative end of the spectrum, there were Evangelicals who escaped back to orthodoxy, so at the radical end there were those who escaped into unstructured free religion. The air was thin, and the company meager, and so only the hardiest, like Abbot, persevered. In the process, however, the boundaries of the denomination were defined.[32]

III

The Radicals were splendid gadflies and dissenters within the denomination, and their influence on it throughout the closing decades of the century was considerable. On their own, however, they showed little sustained constructive power. The main thrust of denominational development rested in the hands of the Broad Church group, which was moving towards a position in which the old line of cleavage between Transcendentalist and non-Transcendentalist no longer mattered. Without one whit abating their reverence for Emerson or their respect for the memory of Parker, Hedge and Clarke found that they had a great deal in common with Hale and Bellows. These men were able to unite for common action on the basis of a cluster of common values, which marked them off both from the Older Rationalists and from those Transcendentalists who went the way of Free Religion. This cluster of attitudes includes: (a) a primary Christian commitment; (b) a strong sense of the importance of the Church as an institution; and (c) an insistence on historical continuities in religion.

At first glance, these men may seem much like the Evangelicals or the Older Rationalists in their Christian commitment. But their commitment actually had a different grounding. In various ways they affirmed the uniqueness of Christianity, while denying that its claims were based on historic evidences. "The divine origin of Christianity must be postulated," Hedge insisted; "it cannot be proved." [33] In the case of Bellows, there may be seen a shift from reliance on "the positive religion of the miracle-working, crucified, risen, ascended Son of God" (1857) to a rejection of miraculous evidences and an assertion that the claims of Christianity and the Church rest solely on their merits: "their fitness to meet the religious wants of their times" (1881).[34] Clarke argued that the real question is not whether Christianity is or is not supernatural, but whether Christianity is "intended by God to be the religion of the human race." It is not disputes about miracles that will answer that question, but the science of comparative religion, by showing that Christianity will replace the other world religions "by teaching all the truth they have taught, and supplying that which they have omitted." [35]

To these men, Christianity was a fact embedded in two millennia of history; and even if one discarded all notions of its supernatural origins, it would still be the indispensable medium through which men and women could best find expression for their religious sentiments and satisfaction for their religious longings. For Joseph Henry Allen, in 1882, it was enough to say:

> The name Christian does not rest, as I hold it, on any theory whatever about the nature or office or person or doctrine of Christ. It rests simply on the fact that we are Christian by habit or inheritance, unless we deliberately choose to renounce that name in favor of some other.[36]

The Broad Church men were not only emphatically Christian; they were committed to the Church. Sometimes this concern finds expression in a criticism of the truncated doctrine of the Church held by members of the older generation: "Is not the notion of *the Church* as distinct from the Churches, pretty much lost out of the N-Eng^d consciousness?" Bellows complained. More frequently, however, he protested the excessive individualism and lack of any genuine corporate sense on the part of the Radicals. "In his individual capacity, as an inorganic, unrelated, independent being," he told the Divinity School alumni, "a man has not, and cannot have, the affections, internal experiences and dispositions, or the powers and blessings, which he can and may, and will receive in his corporate capacity . . ." Rejecting alike Radicalism as "thin, ghostly individualism," and Boston conservatism as "meagre congregationalism," he sought to reanimate the

Church by heartily recognizing "the existing religious institutions of Christendom as the chosen channel through which the divine Word is seeking to descend into Humanity and the world." [37]

Hedge's commitment to the Church—that is to say, the Christian Church, not just a handful of New England Unitarian churches, let alone a self-sufficient "free church" here and there—was equally emphatic. "The Church does not exist by the will of man," he wrote, "but by his constitution. It cannot be abolished by the will of man; it cannot perish by disaffection." It was not abolished by the Transcendentalists: "the Church that was present then, and was judged moribund by transcendental zeal, and rattled so ominously in transcendental ears, is present still." Nor will it be supplanted, as the Free Religionists may suppose, by associations of rational thinkers devoted to Theism in the abstract. There is a difference between a Church and a school of religious philosophy. "A Church is the embodiment of a spiritual force, which, sallying from the heart of God, creates a vortex in human society that compels the kingdoms, compels the aeons, in its conquering wake, and tracks its way through the world with a shining psychopomp of stately souls." [38]

The note of criticism of extreme individualism in religion—the individualism that shies away from coöperative action lest a person's integrity be somehow diminished thereby—recurs repeatedly. "Our great foe is Individualism, born of Protestant Freedom," Clarke complained. "The social and corporate element in our religious system is very weak." He himself was not interested in counteracting this tendency by developing a common liturgy, as Bellows was; or by emphasis on a common creed, or on common emotionalism as in a revival meeting. But he was much concerned to develop union through common practical endeavor, and it was in this frame of mind that he addressed the New York convention: "It is not a meeting for speculation or discussion,—it is a meeting for *work*. It is a meeting of churches who think the time has come for organized work, and who know that individual work is work at random, while organized work is work which tells." Where Emerson had once prescribed "first, soul, and second, soul, and evermore, soul," Clarke responded: "Soul is good, but body is good, too." [39]

The historical consciousness of the Broad Church men also sets them apart both from the Older Rationalists and from the free religionist variety of Transcendentalist. To be sure, the Older Rationalists had insisted that Christianity was an historical religion whose claims are rooted in the appearance of Jesus Christ as an historical event. But the function performed by Christ was to be the vehicle of divine revelation, and that revelation itself was not relative to any historical situation. Indeed, the role of the biblical critic was to penetrate the historical particularities of the biblical account in order to disclose the pure and unconditioned revelation beyond. For the supernatural rationalist, there was no compelling logic that required the revelation of God through Christ to have occurred at the time and place in history that it did. Despite all the talk of historical evidences, Supernatural Rationalism was basically anti-historical.

For Emerson and Parker, too, history is something to be transcended rather than embraced. Emerson put an essay on "History" first in *Essays: First Series*. But it was the "universal nature" revealed in history that concerned him, not "particular men and things." Inspiration, the intuition of the divine, the "one Fact, the one and only good news"—all these are for him things "above time." In comparable fashion, for Parker, Absolute Religion is as universal as the nature of man; it is the reality that must be grasped, though obscured by transient historical forms.

But men like Bellows, Hedge, and Clarke could not avoid thinking in developmental terms, rather than simply in terms of abstract absolutes, whether rationalistic or transcendental. Issues in theology that an earlier generation would have measured against the standards of Reason, or a nonhistorical understanding of scripture, now were treated genetically. Orthodox doctrines were no longer wrong doctrines to be argued down or serenely ignored, but were to be sympathetically understood as expressions of immature but necessary phases of belief, which even yet may contain something of value. Evolution, transformation, development, history, progress—these were among the prevailing motifs of the nineteenth century; and the Broad Church men were alert and sensitive to them.

Thus Bellows acknowledged that he was of necessity a representative of the nineteenth century, a "child of the age." But other ages had "their spirit, their truths, and their experience"; they have left "their wealth and wisdom as our inheritance." Our peril, he said, especially in America, derives from "a disrespect and forgetfulness of the past, a contempt for the institutions that transmit its life, an isolation in self-complacency, a rash abandonment of the conquests, the experience, and the truths of Humanity historically studied and integrated." [40]

Even more than Bellows, Hedge, by a lifetime of concern, represents the historical-mindedness of the Broad Church group, since he was professor of ecclesiastical history at the Divinity School for twenty years. Indeed it was his sense of history, more than anything else, that set him apart from Transcendentalists like Emerson, even at the beginning. Recalling, thirty years later, the gatherings of the Transcendental Club, or "Hedge's Club," which he hugely enjoyed, he acknowledged that even then he had no faith in ecclesiastical revolutions based on the assumption that a fresh start could make the past irrelevant. He always discerned "a power and meaning in the old," which some of his associates would not acknowledge. He had made up his mind that "the method of revolution in theology is not discession, but development." In short: "My historical consciousness, then as since, balanced my neology, and kept me ecclesiastically conservative, though intellectually radical." [41]

Steeped as he was in the writings of the German Idealists, there was very much of a Hegelian flavor to Hedge's treatment of the Church as unfolding God's will in history. "You cannot think more highly than I do of the historic importance of Xy," he wrote to Bellows in 1856.

> To me also it is no accidental development, nor mere human product, but a divine manifestation—God in history . . . But you will agree with me that Xy is a process & not a finality, a progressive development, not a formalized summary of the Spirit. And therefore the balance of Xy is likely to be with the progressive minds in the church. Only they must be *in* the Church and not out of it. [42]

IV

Unitarian history from 1865 to 1894 should not be told solely in terms of conflict and factional dispute. In the local churches, ministers were occupied with the pastoral care of their congregations; and in meetings of the National Conference or the A.U.A., delegates worked without rancor on all sorts of common enterprises. Most of the life of the churches, and of the denomination, was not controversial—or, if controversial, not divisive. Yet there were nagging unresolved issues that repeatedly intruded. If the conflicts over these issues should not be exaggerated, neither may they be overlooked.

The underlying issue for a generation continued to be the self-identity of Unitarianism: whether it would be defined in exclusively Christian terms, as the more conservative wished; or in predominantly Christian terms, though with room for the Radicals, as the Broad Church group preferred; or in non-Christian terms, though with considerable Christian content, as the Radicals desired.

This underlying issue surfaced repeatedly, especially in discussions over statements of faith, or other forms of words, that might be taken to define the limits of acceptable Unitarian belief. The more conservative Unitarians wanted a rather specific statement of Christian supernaturalism; and while they sincerely disavowed any intent to use such a statement as a creedal test, they would have made it hard for any free religionist to feel that a generous welcome was extended. The Radicals, on the other hand, were sticklers when it came to traditional language, and saw creedalism in a reference to the obligation of "disciples of the Lord Jesus Christ to prove their faith by self-denial," even when accompanied by the general proviso that decisions and resolutions of the National Conference should be understood as expressive of the opinion of the majority only, "committing in no degree those who object to them." [43] In between the conservatives and the Radicals, spokesmen for the Broad Church group tried to argue that common action was more necessary than agreement on doctrinal statements; but that if the denomination were to develop the coherence needed for effective action, some indication as to where it stood doctrinally would be desirable, and it was true to the facts for the Unitarians to describe their body as normatively— though not exclusively—Christian.

From 1865 to 1894, the denomination labored to reconcile the several points of view regarding the identity of Unitarianism, and to state it in such a way as to be acceptable to all factions. The issue was fought through in three distinct arenas: the National Conference, the A.U.A., and the Western Conference.

(1) *The National Conference.* The New York convention had seen the triumph of the Broad Church group, led by Bellows. Not everyone was pleased with his new ecclesiasticism, however. There were conservatives who still wanted a more explicit creedal statement; and there were Radicals who complained that the preamble, if not a creed, was at least a creedlet. In the next few years, both wings sought to force a restatement of the basis for the Conference in terms more to their own liking.

The first attempt was made by certain of the Radicals, led by Francis Ellingwood Abbot. He had been disappointed by the sectarian name and conservative preamble of the Conference; but he was by no means as hostile, at that time, as was Octavius Brooks Frothingham. In reporting the doings of the convention to his own parish, he noted that the temper of the convention had been "unmistakably opposed to creeds in any form," and he told his radical colleagues that they were "decidedly in the wrong" when they interpreted the preamble as a creed.[44]

Abbot went to the second meeting of the Conference at Syracuse in 1866, with a revised version, which would have defined the Christianity of the Conference in terms of the universal diffusion of Love, Righteousness, and Truth, instead of discipleship to Christ. The preamble as it stood, he argued, was regarded by the Radicals as a sort of creed; it contained, at least by implication, a doctrine of the Lordship of Christ to which they could not subscribe. A revision would enable them to work with the Conference with good conscience.[45]

Resistance to Abbot's amendment was expressed on several grounds. Dr. Hedge took issue with the definition: "Christianity," he said, "in any admissable sense of the term, cannot be disengaged from the Christ of the record, the unfathomable Christ of the Gospel."[46] James Freeman Clarke pointed out that Abbot's amendment took a position on disputed issues of theology, and it could just as easily be criticized as being a creed as the preamble it would replace. Clarke and Dr. Samuel Osgood agreed that the proposed new version might have been accepted had it been offered a year earlier; but now to revise the preamble would seem to be to refuse to recognize Christ as the head of the Church. Some delegates, like Samuel J. May, complained that the Conference ought to be about its practical business instead of spending time on endless and fruitless talk; it was, after all, an organization for work, not for the refinement of theological distinctions. After extended debate, Abbot's proposal was defeated by a large majority.

The prevailing view as the meeting closed was that the majority had won after a fair opportunity for serious discussion carried on at an honorable level of civilized debate. Expressing the dominant opinion of the denomination, the Conference had reaffirmed its Christian identity at the center, but would not define its perimeter by means of creedal tests and exclusions. But defeated minorities view such matters in a different light than successful majorities do. Abbot felt that what had been defeated were the principles of perfect spiritual freedom and universal spiritual fellowship, and that, regardless of what spokesmen for the majority might say, the Radicals had been "at last definitely excluded from the only organization from which they could expect the affirmation of their own great principles." [47]

Shortly after the Syracuse meeting, therefore, a small group of the Radicals met at the home of Dr. Cyrus A. Bartol of the West Church in Boston, to see what might be done to advance the cause of complete spiritual freedom. Some of the participants, Abbot among them, wanted a new organization; others, like Bartol and Samuel Johnson, basically anti-institutional in temperament, were inclined to argue that participation in any organization was of necessity a limitation on individual spiritual liberty. Those in favor of organization decided to go ahead, with the acquiescence though not the active participation of the individualists. Among those they recruited to the cause was Octavius Brooks Frothingham, "whose name alone was felt to be worth a thousand men." [48]

The result was the formation at a public meeting in May, 1867, of the Free Religious Association. It was an organization of individuals, not a denomination or quasi-denomination. Most of its clerical members retained their standing with the denomination, serving as ministers of Unitarian churches and participating in the work of the A.U.A. and the National Conference. It sought to be broader than Unitarianism by enlisting free spirits from many denominations, but only a few such became active in its affairs; so it was chiefly a focal point for discussion and exchange of views among Radicals within Unitarianism. Its members were highly verbal, and devoted their efforts to public meetings, lectures, the distribution of tracts, the publication of books, and the sponsorship of magazines. The membership list was never large, and the core of devoted workers was very small; but for those who were deeply involved, it was one of the major commitments of their lives, and even in recollection, every detail of its beginnings and early years seemed of momentous historical significance. It began with a burst of energy, which lasted about a decade; thereafter the meetings became more and more perfunctory and the amount of publication diminished. The Association lasted long enough to celebrate its fiftieth anniversary, but finally faded away without there being any terminal date.[49]

After the Syracuse meeting, delegates to the National Conference continued to tinker with its Constitution in an attempt to find a formula satisfactory to both conservatives and Radicals. In 1868, a new article was added, stating that all declarations of the Conference, including the preamble, were "expressions only of its majority, committing in no degree those who object to them." [50] The Radicals reacted scornfully, arguing that it was patently absurd to have a preamble that no one was obliged to respect. In 1870, a more conservative substitute was passed, inviting to fellowship "all who wish to be followers of Christ";[51] predictably the Radicals regarded this as a reaffirmation of creedal Christianity. In 1882, a further attempt was made to restate the balance between a Christian identity and openness to other points of view, and a new Article X was adopted almost unanimously, this time on motion by Minot J. Savage, who was one of those active in the F.R.A.:

> While we believe that the Preamble and Articles of our Constitution fairly represent the opinions of the majority of our churches, yet we wish, distinctly, to put on record our declaration that they are no authoritative test of Unitarianism, and are not intended to exclude from our fellowship any who, while differing from us in belief, are in general sympathy with our purposes and practical aims.[52]

Bellows, now dead, would surely have applauded; in debate,

both Edward Everett Hale and James Freeman Clarke declared that this had been their understanding from the beginning as to the basis for the Conference.

(2) *The A.U.A.* Meanwhile, the same issue emerged in the affairs of the A.U.A. Two episodes attracted wide attention: the Hepworth resolution in 1870, and the Year Book controversy in 1873.

George H. Hepworth was one of the more "evangelical" of the ministers, who was especially sensitive to the problems involved in attracting to Unitarianism restless members of more orthodox churches. If we had an authorized statement of what Liberal Christianity stands for, he argued, many displaced liberals from other denominations might join. In 1870, therefore, he came to the May meetings of the A.U.A. with a proposal that a special committee be appointed "*t*o prepare and present . . . to this body, for its approval and indorsement, a statement of faith, which shall, as nearly as may be, represent the religious opinions of the Unitarian denomination." [53]

Hepworth had been in active consultation with Bellows prior to the meeting, and believed that he had his hearty support, since Bellows had many times urged the usefulness of such statements, so long as they were without binding authority. Much to Hepworth's surprise, however, Bellows spoke against the proposal in terms that made him sound almost like a Radical. "I say, sir," Bellows exclaimed, "that the Christian religion at this present time needs a body which will restrain itself, and not undertake to bind itself by a positive statement which will strangle its growth." [54] Hepworth always felt that Bellows had let him down, influenced at the last moment by pressures from the Radicals. Perhaps no one will ever be able to explain precisely what happened in the innermost recesses of Bellows's mind. As an inveterate mediator, he may have felt that at that juncture it was the Radicals who needed to be conciliated. He was devoted equally to Unitarian Christianity and to freedom in religion; he was mercurial in temper, and sometimes seemed inconsistent as he stressed first one of the principles and then the other. Yet he thereby expressed the dilemma of his generation of Unitarians. But his speech was long remembered for its devastating impact on the Hepworth proposal. "I can never forget," wrote John White

Chadwick, three decades later, "the effective manner in which Drs. Hedge and Bellows gave the movement its quietus at the annual meeting of the Association. . . . Here was one instance of many where the brunt of the illiberal and reactionary tendency was withstood by men of conservative thought and feeling." [55]

The Year Book controversy was an episode into which the denomination stumbled almost inadvertently. The Year Book regularly listed the Unitarian churches and their ministers, but this compilation was for convenience only, and had no official status. The ministers were those who were understood to be Unitarians, not those whose credentials had been approved by a fellowship committee or similar body. In 1873, Octavius Brooks Frothingham noted that his name was included, even though his church had declared itself to be an independent one, and he himself was now committed to Free Religion. He therefore asked that his name be removed. The assistant secretary of the Association, George W. Fox, then wondered whether other names were improperly included, and wrote to half-a-dozen of Frothingham's associates to inquire if their names were listed "with their knowledge and consent."

Among those to whom he wrote was the Reverend William J. Potter of New Bedford, the secretary of the F.R.A. Potter replied that his name was indeed there with his knowledge and consent; that he did not agree with Frothingham that members of the F.R.A. should request their names to be withdrawn. But the list, he noted, was drawn up by officers of the Association, using their own criteria for inclusion, and it was for them to decide whether his name should be dropped. Fox doubtless breathed a sigh of relief, and wrote back that he was glad to know that Potter could still be listed as "one who calls himself a Unitarian Christian." [56]

There had been a tendency among members of the F.R.A. to move to a narrow and rigorous definition of the word "Christian," instead of a broad and accommodating one; and so, in reply, Potter felt compelled to make it plain that he did not call himself a Unitarian Christian. " 'Christian,' of course, I am with respect to the doctrine of the Trinity. But 'Christian' I do not now call myself, and have so said in public." Thereupon, Fox reached the conclusion that Potter's name should be dropped after all.[57]

Predictably, the Radicals pointed to this act as another example of Unitarian bigotry, while conservatives took satisfaction in this reinforcement of the Christian identity of the denomination. But the issue was not all that simple. There was, in the first place, the matter of the unofficial character of the listing, in a publication of the A.U.A., which was still a voluntary organization of individuals. There was the long-standing lack of clarity as to the basis for inclusion—whether, for example, any minister serving a church generally regarded as Unitarian should be listed without question. There was the lack of consensus as to the definition of the term "Unitarian Christian," even if one admitted that this was a legitimate standard for inclusion. There was the universal esteem in which Potter was held, even by those who were far from being Radicals, or admirers of Abbot and Frothingham. There was the irony of the fact that Potter was and continued to be a life member of the A.U.A., one of whose officers had in effect disfellowshipped him. Little wonder that the discussions of the episode produced peculiar alignments. Hedge and Clarke thought that Potter had defined himself out of the Christian ministry; but Charles Lowe, who was at least as conservative as they, and a former secretary of the A.U.A. besides, deplored Fox's action, arguing that the Year Book should offer a factual listing of those former secretary of the A.U.A. besides, deplored Fox's action, of the Association, declaring that he would not "stand watchdog to keep any away from our enclosure, slight as are our barriers to keep out intruders." [59]

The action of the assistant secretary was sustained by the Executive Committee of the A.U.A., and then by the members at the annual meeting in May, 1874. At the National Conference meeting in September, Bellows introduced a motion endorsing the action of the Conference in extending the customary invitation to Potter's church to be present "by its pastor and lay delegates"; but the Conference shied away from such an endorsement of Potter, and the motion was tabled.[60] In 1883, to the regular list of Unitarian ministers in the Year Book there was appended a short "Additional List," including Potter's name; and in 1884, apparently without comment or protest, the two lists were consolidated.

(3) *The Western Conference.* In 1886 and for several years thereafter, the locus of controversy was the Western Conference,

where the debate was referred to as "The Western Issue," or "The Issue in the West." The radical wing of the Western Conference were commonly called the "Unity men," because the magazine *Unity* was their organ; and their position was often termed "the ethical basis," since they proposed to define Unitarianism in terms of "freedom, fellowship, and character" in religion, with no explicit reference either to theism or to Christianity. Their leading spokesmen were Jenkin Lloyd Jones of Chicago and William Channing Gannett of St. Paul. Most prominent of the Christian wing of the Conference was Jabez T. Sunderland of Ann Arbor.

The Western Conference dated from 1852. Like the National Conference, it had always included delegates from churches; but like the A.U.A., it had carried on a considerable amount of missionary activity, with at least a part-time field representative. In some degree, therefore, its functions overlapped both of the other organizations; but its existence was justified by its distance from Boston and the tendency of the A.U.A. to become absorbed in problems closer at hand. Indeed, an arrangement in the early 1870s by which the A.U.A. took over all missionary activity almost put an end to western expansion and nearly killed the Western Conference. It was resurrected, however, and Jenkin Lloyd Jones served as its secretary and field representative from 1875 to 1884.

When Jones resigned as secretary, Sunderland was chosen to take his place. His first annual report, in 1885, expressed concern because Unitarianism in the West was not expanding as rapidly as the population. "Actually it grows, slowly," he wrote; "but relatively it does not." The reason, he felt, was the refusal of Unitarianism to state positively the basis for the movement; in other words, its disinclination to come to grips with the theological principles it stood for. "We have tried to make our movement so broad that its constant tendency has been to lose all cohesiveness, or significance, or inspiration, or power, or value." Or, more pointedly: "We have tried to be so inclusive of every possible class of religious believers, and especially non-believers, that the result has been in many cases the practical exclusion of the believers." While he had no intention of proposing a formal creed, let alone a creedal test, he did think Unitarians should stand on a platform; and his proposal was "the matchless summary of religious duty which comes to us from Jesus: Love of God and love to man." As

Henry Whitney Bellows

Octavius Brooks Frothingham

Frederic Henry Hedge

Jenkin Lloyd Jones

a practical proposal, he recommended that the secretary of the Western Conference also serve as the western agent of the A.U.A., which would pay a part of his salary. While some of the westerners were fearful of entanglements with the "conservative" A.U.A., practical considerations prevailed, and Sunderland undertook to act in both capacities.[61]

Confrontation between the two wings came at the meeting of the Conference at Cincinnati in 1886. Shortly before the meeting, Sunderland distributed a 45-page pamphlet entitled *The Issue in the West*, in which he elaborated further the concerns he had expressed in his 1885 report. The tenor of the argument is indicated by the questions posed on the title page: "Is Western Unitarianism Ready to Give Up Its Christian Character? Is It Ready to Give Up Its Theistic Character?" He took his stand in opposition to "that party of good and loved but singularly misjudging men" who step by step had been seeking to move Unitarianism from a Christian basis to one of Free Religion.[62]

In the business meeting of the Conference, Sunderland proposed the following resolution: "That, while rejecting all creeds and creed limitations, the Western Unitarian Conference hereby expresses its purpose as a body to be the promotion of a religion of love to god and love to man." He explained that he had deliberately omitted the word "Christian" as perhaps offensive to some. Nevertheless, the resolution was defeated, by a margin of about 20 to 34, as were other resolutions with similar intent offered by the Christian Unitarians. On the other hand, by a vote of 34 to 10, the Conference passed a resolution offered by Gannett: "That the Western Unitarian Conference conditions its fellowship on no dogmatic tests, but welcomes all who wish to join it to help establish truth, righteousness and love in the world." [63]

Since Sunderland opposed creeds and creedal tests, while Gannett was himself a reverent theist—and certainly not a rejector of Christianity, after the mode of Francis Ellingwood Abbot—one might have supposed that an accommodation could have been reached. But certain of the words of the resolutions had taken on a symbolic meaning far beyond their usual intellectual content. For the conservatives it was a matter of significance that Gannett's resolution carefully eliminated the words "the kingdom of God," which had been used in a similar resolution in 1875; this, they felt, was an example of the way the Unity men had persistently and over a period of years sought to "bleach" out all theistic and Christian language.[64] Besides, although the meetings were carried on with good temper on all sides, personalities and personal antagonisms affected the outcome. Joseph H. Crooker of Madison, who thought the controversy a needless one, was critical of the leading spokesmen of both factions: "In reality, all the trouble has come from Gannett's finical objection to the phrase: 'kingdom of God' and Sunderland's mistaken dogmatism." [65]

Whether needless or not, the controversy was a real one. The conservatives had already felt it necessary, in order to get a hearing, to establish a journal of their own as a counterbalance to *Unity*. Now, meeting in Chicago in June, 1886, they organized a new Western Unitarian Association as a western auxiliary of the A.U.A. Conservatives urged the A.U.A. to reappoint Sunderland as its western agent; the Unity men argued for the appointment of J. R. Effinger, the new secretary of the Western Conference. But the officers of the A.U.A. preferred to heed western men like Crooker and T. B. Forbush, who advised a neutral course, giving encouragement to neither faction. As Forbush put it: "Hence arises, it seems to me, the wisdom of masterly inactivity until this squall blows over and those who are active in it begin [to] get cool & perhaps feel a little ashamed." [66]

Apart from the questions of factionalism and personalities, the problem confronting Western Unitarianism was the perennial one with which Unitarians East and West had grappled since the New York convention of 1865. It was how to make a descriptive, or even normative, statement of the Unitarian position in a way that would express the predominantly Christian loyalties of the denomination, without opening the way for its use as a creedal test, or basis of exclusion. That was what Bellows sought; it was what Sunderland wanted; and it was what Gannett himself finally tried to accomplish. "Very well," he said, "why should not Unitarians at last combine and make that public affirmation, but in such a way that it shall be *impossible* for themselves or any one around to treat it as a 'creed'? " [67]

Gannett therefore prepared for the 1887 meeting of the Western Conference an omnibus resolution, which combined the 1886 statement rejecting dogmatic tests with a new statement of

"Things Most Commonly Believed To-day Among Us." With respect to the point on which the conservatives were most sensitive, Gannett asserted that with few exceptions, Unitarians "may be called Christian theists; theists, as worshipping the One-in-All, and naming that One, 'God, our Father'; Christian, because revering Jesus as the greatest of the historic prophets of religion." [68] This was passed by the 1887 meeting, the vote being 59 to 13; though it is to be noted that Sunderland and many of the other conservatives were not in attendance. His position on the matter was that, while the Western Conference, or the A.U.A., or the National Conference should properly define in its constitution what its own purposes were, it was presumptuous for any such conference to make an official pronouncement as to what the views of a majority of Unitarians were understood to be.

Yet it is clear that the doctrinal or ideological basis for reconciliation was present, and the will to achieve it existed among many Unitarians who felt that the discussion had degenerated into trivial verbal distinctions, compounded by stubborn likes and dislikes with respect to the use of particular words. The issue continued to fester for several years, like a low-grade infection. Then, in 1892, Sunderland suggested that those who held his position would be satisfied if the Western Conference were to add a clause to Gannett's "Statement," to the effect that the purpose of the Conference was "to promulgate a religion in harmony with the foregoing preamble and statement." [69] Younger men in the West, notably W. W. Fenn of Chicago and S. M. Crothers of St. Paul, who had not been involved in the earlier wrangling, strongly supported this way out of the tangle. Gannett and the other members of what had now become the intransigent "old guard" resisted any tampering with their handiwork, but were voted down, 42 to 27. A new generation was emerging, no longer willing to be immobilized by the linguistic scruples of Gannett, or to accept the domination of the Conference by "boss Jones," or, for that matter, to share Sunderland's anxieties about the neglect of the Christian name.[70]

(4) *The National Conference Again.* Meanwhile, a further revision of the Constitution of the National Conference was under consideration. In 1891, a committee to review the matter was authorized, of which Edward Everett Hale became chairman.

Early in 1894, it tried its hand at devising a new formula that might be acceptable to both wings of the denomination. Letters to the editor, pro and con, began to appear in the *Christian Register*. At the National Conference in September at Saratoga, an informal meeting was called prior to the business meeting to permit discussion of the various proposals that had been advanced; and much to the surprise of everyone, a consensus began to emerge in support of a modified version of the committee proposal. As finally presented to the business session of the Conference, it took this form:

> These churches accept the religion of Jesus, holding, in accordance with his teaching, that practical religion is summed up in love to God and love to man. The Conference recognizes the fact that its constituency is Congregational in tradition and polity. Therefore, it declares that nothing in this constitution is to be construed as an authoritative test; and we cordially invite to our working fellowship any who, while differing from us in belief, are in general sympathy with our spirit and our practical aims.[71]

When the question was put by the presiding officer, a chorus of "ayes" was heard. The nays were called for; there was a breathless silence; not a single voice was heard in opposition; then thunderous applause and shouts of joy broke out. "No cold type can picture the enthusiasm which followed," reported the editor of the *Register*; while the editor of *The Unitarian* described the scene thus: "Many clasped hands; while others, who remembered similar debates with sadly different results, shed tears of gratitude. Such a scene has never occurred before in the history of Unitarianism. All disputes disappeared in faith, all wrangling in love, all individual idiosyncrasies were hushed in the one great holy spirit of God's peace." [72]

A generation's search for consensus was over. And the happiest aspect of it was that it was a genuine consensus, so that as the denomination confronted the Twentieth Century it was more united than it had been for two generations, since the time of Emerson's Divinity School Address. T. B. Forbush's comment was a just one: "No victory, no compromise, but just a coming together on a higher level. Nobody surrendered anything, but all said this is just what we mean." Or, as Samuel J. Barrows put it: "In this matter there was no pitiful compromise, no bargaining, no cutting and trimming: no conviction was suppressed or abated. The joyful spontaneity with which the declaration was accepted, the warm and generous enthusiasm with which it was ratified, left no trace of seam or faction." [73]

V

The Saratoga Conference ended thirty years of controversy. Yet the final outcome was substantially what Bellows had sought at the New York convention in 1865. Why was it possible to achieve consensus without compromise in 1894, when the struggle had been so prolonged and at times so acrimonious? A combination of factors must be acknowledged here.

In the first place, the interplay of personalities was affected by the passage of time, so that spokesmen for the two extreme positions, particularly those of an uncompromising temper or rigid personality structure, lost influence. Francis Ellingwood Abbot took himself out of the denomination at one side, as

"Old" Twenty-five Beacon Street offices of A.U.A.

Bookroom in "old 25."

George Hepworth did at the other. Jenkin Lloyd Jones found himself increasingly in a marginal position at the radical end of the spectrum, while some of the more conservative men, like Rufus Ellis and Edmund Hamilton Sears became parish men who steered clear of active denominational involvement. In some instances, a mellowing took place with age: Octavius Brooks Frothingham, in the closing years of his life, after ill health made it necessary for him to leave the active ministry, often attended services at the First Church in Boston, of which Rufus Ellis and then Stopford Brooke were ministers. The denomination was engaged in a subtle process of definition of boundaries by which Abbot was out but Potter was in; Hepworth was out but Sunderland was in.

Related to this process of self-definition, there was, in the second place, a growing denominational consciousness, as Bellows had hoped. This in turn is related to the increased visibility and effectiveness of denominational organization, with the A.U.A. coming more and more to be the stable support for such activities as church extension and ministerial settlement. In this period, the Association was well served by its secretaries, particularly Charles Lowe and Grindall Reynolds, and by its long-term professional bureaucrat, George W. Fox. Their day-in-and-day-out devotion to the work of the Association had an incalculable cumulative effect on the way in which Unitarians generally thought of their local churches in relationship to the denomination.

This was also a period in which, at both the local and the national level, the churches were developing new instruments for common activity, such as the Women's Auxiliary Conference, which later became the Women's Alliance.[74] Then, in 1886, the denomination for the first time acquired a headquarters building designed especially for its use. The construction of the original 25 Beacon Street provided not only office space, meeting rooms, and a lecture hall, but a visible, tangible testimony to the growing importance of the A.U.A. in the life of the denomination.[75] Unlike the F.R.A., or Jenkin Lloyd Jones's Congress of Religious Liberals, which were extensions of the personalities of their leading spirits, the A.U.A. was developing an institutional life and momentum of its own, which, as it was involved in contacts with ministers and lay people in the churches, was formed by and in turn helped to shape the characteristic style of the denomination.

Finally, the second half of the nineteenth century was marked by an accelerated tendency in Western thought to interpret phenomena in historical or developmental terms, and no religious body was more sensitive to this tendency than the Unitarians. They were receptive to it in many different forms and manifestations: evolutionary thought, Spencerian or Darwinian; German Idealism, particularly with a Hegelian flavoring; Biblical criticism, which gave a developmental account of the shaping of the Bible, and a persuasive reconstruction of the history of the religion of Israel; a version of the eighteenth-century idea of progress, which, to be sure, could be vulgarized into praise of material growth or support of Manifest Destiny; romantic notions of human nature, in which the capacity for spiritual growth was considered to be innate in every individual, a concept likewise subject to vulgarization at Unitarian hands, in the novels of the Reverend Horatio Alger, Jr.

These concepts, often in their better, sometimes in their worse forms were assimilated without difficulty, across the whole range of Unitarian groups and factions: there is no significant difference, for example, between the reception of Darwinian evolution by Radicals and by conservatives. This developmental way of looking at religious ideas and institutions undercut equally the Absolute

Religion of Theodore Parker and the static rationalism of Andrews Norton. The conflict between Christian Theist and Free Religionist was not eliminated, but its sharpness was moderated, by an infusion of historical relativism. By emphasizing the relationship to Christianity as one of cherished historical continuity, rather than adherence to particular doctrinal formulations, the denomination avoided serious internal disruption as it moved into an age of secularism in which Christian motifs were increasingly bleached out of American Protestantism generally. More important for Unitarians at the close of the century than their long-standing differences was the common acceptance of an all-pervasive evolutionary optimism, so that conservative and radical alike could join in accepting at least the fifth of James Freeman Clarke's Five Points of Unitarian Belief: "The progress of mankind onward and upward forever."

Chapter 4

"A Wave at Crest"

Administration Reform,

and Depression, 1898-1934

I

In January, 1898, the five boroughs of greater New York were consolidated into New York City. Although no one may have realized it at the time, an event of comparable importance to Unitarians occurred in Boston that same month. Samuel A. Eliot became secretary and chief executive officer of the American Unitarian Association.

Eliot, thirty-five years of age, united in himself the energies of Boston Unitarianism, Harvard liberalism, European urbanity, pioneer zeal, and concern for oppressed peoples. His paternal grandfather was Samuel A. Eliot (for whom he was named), congressman, mayor of Boston, and a founder of the American Unitarian Association; his maternal grandfather was the Reverend Ephraim Peabody, minister of King's Chapel. Eliot's father, Charles W. Eliot, had been elected president of Harvard College in March, 1869, when the boy was six; tragically, his mother died the day after the election, with the result that a remarkable closeness developed between father and son, which was to last fifty-seven years.[1] Young Eliot had travelled in Europe as a young man, preferring "unsystematic excursions," as he called them, to formal classroom learning.[2] As a new Harvard graduate, he had spent part of a year as a Unitarian missionary in the Pacific Northwest, visiting existing churches, starting new ones, and surveying the needs and prospects of the denomination. In his travels, he had also observed the wretched living conditions of native Americans in the Northwest and of southern blacks in Virginia and Alabama; his ministry and administrative vision always included these diminished peoples.

The secretary of the A.U.A. was the association's chief administrative official. The position had been created in 1832, seven years after the founding, when it was realized that the job of part-time secretary was incompatible with parish duties. "This office of Secretary is the head and front of the Association," said the Reverend Samuel K. Lothrop, the president, in 1854.[3] The secretary was a missionary agent responsible for overseeing churches, settling ministers, distributing literature, and implementing decisions of the board of directors.

When the Reverend George Batchelor resigned the secretaryship in November, 1897, to become editor of the *Christian Register*,[4] Eliot was the obvious replacement. A director since 1894, he was the most vigorous and creative member of the board. His ministries in Denver (1889-1892), where, stimulated by the silver boom, the population trebled to 106,000 during the 1880s,[5] and thereafter in Brooklyn, where he had quickly moved to the front rank of Protestant clergy,[6] had given Eliot experience and visibility. So effective an organizer was he—of churches, regional conferences, and charitable institutions—that the Reverend William Wallace Fenn, an A.U.A. director who was minister of the First Unitarian Church of Chicago, opposed his election because of fear of centralization.[7]

Eliot's mandate to the A.U.A. on his election was simple enough: "We must have a concentration of responsible authority and a responsible executive." [8] Frustrated when, as a Unitarian missionary in Seattle, he had in 1888 sought building loan assistance from the Association, Eliot wrote: "The present . . . lack of system . . . can readily be amended by the introduction of more precise business methods into the management of the A.U.A." Then he added: "A corporation managed by ministers needs business discipline more than work." [9] As a director he had advocated a pay-as-you-go policy on current income, permanent investment of bequests, and a consolidated portfolio. Possessing the reins of power, he moved to implement his proposals. At his bidding, the directors instituted a reversionary clause in all building loans and grants-in-aid.[10] They voted that "no appropriation shall be made to any society that is in arrears to the Church Building Loan Fund." They authorized collective investment of funds.

The Association prospered under Eliot's hand. Current income rose from $52,000 to $58,000 in one year, capital gifts from $7,000 to $40,000.[11] In May, 1899, he was able to report "marked improvements . . . in the methods of conducting the business of the Association." On the basis of his travels to all parts of the continent, he added that the "work is genuinely national, alike in vision and performance." [12]

So singular was Eliot's leadership that when, in January, 1900, he received a call from Boston's South Congregational Church to succeed the Reverend Edward Everett Hale, the directors voted to change the constitution to grant Eliot "the opportunity for service that he desires." [13] Encouraged by supportive letters in the *Register*—one declared: "we need his organizing power" [14]—Eliot declined the call, his decision itself prompting a gift of $5,000 to the Association.

In April, 1900, the president, the Honorable Carroll D. Wright, declined renomination, urging that the president should be "an active executive officer." [15] The nominating committee recommended reorganization of the executive staff and nominated "the present secretary" for president of the Association. The 75th annual meeting, jubilant at the oversubscription of a $75,000 anniversary campaign, approved the reorganization and elected Eliot as president. "It will take a generation," wrote Francis Greenwood Peabody, "to disclose how large a work you are doing for us." [16] How right he was!

II

In January, 1900, there were 457 Unitarian churches in North America, two-thirds of them (301) in New England. Of these New England societies, two-thirds (204) were in towns of 10,000 population or less. New England, the *Register* noted, is "practically the only section of the country in which such a thing as rural Unitarianism exists." Eight societies had been added during 1899, in Adrian and Spring Valley, Minnesota; Dunkirk, New York; Highland Springs, Virginia; Newington, New Hampshire; Ord, Nebraska; Pueblo, Colorado; and Goldsboro, Maine.[17] The preeminence of Boston in the Unitarian firmament is indicated by the fact that in 1900 the sixty Unitarian churches within ten miles of the Massachusetts state house contributed nearly half of the A.U.A.'s current income.[18]

"President Eliot occupied the chair." [19] As president, Eliot presided at all business meetings of the Association, including the board of directors and the annual meeting. He was elected annually on nomination of the directors. He appointed all standing committees, including the nominating committee.

Eliot set himself to reordering the work of the Association. He inaugurated "Association Day," an annual recognition by the churches of the denomination's missionary purposes. He launched special inquiries, utilizing the circular letter to the churches, into church attendance, the sources of the ministry, church architecture, and interfaith coöperation. In order to assess "the nature and aim of modern preaching in the liberal churches," Eliot asked every settled minister to submit his subject and text for Sunday, October 20, 1901. He raised the question of the Unitarian name: was it appropriate? One respondent proposed that the denomination call itself: The Universal Church. Building on his lifelong interest in music, he appointed himself chairman of a committee on the improvement of church music; the Reverend John Haynes Holmes, minister of the Third Religious Society in Dorchester, was secretary. Eliot secured a full-time publications agent to develop and distribute free literature. He was midwife in the birthing of the Pacific Unitarian School for the Ministry (now the Starr King School), the Tuckerman School in Boston for training parish assistants, and the Hackley School, a secondary school in Tarrytown, New York. In 1903, he arranged for a chartered train, the "Unitarian Atlantic City Special," to take New England delegates to the National Conference in New Jersey (one-way fare was $9, with parlor-car seat an additional $1.75).[20]

The heart of Eliot's program was missions. "We Unitarians," he declared, "have never sufficiently learned the art of irrigation. We have failed to adequately spread the good news." [21] The basic missionary instrument was the grant-in-aid. At the turn of the century, the A.U.A. aided eighty-nine churches in the amount of $40,000.[22] Shortly Eliot realized the futility of the practice, and the directors voted in 1903 that "the policy of granting continuous aid to dependent churches be gradually and judiciously discontinued and that where appropriations are continued . . . they be . . . concentrated on promising or important enterprises." [23] Believing state universities to be "the most powerful instruments for the upbuilding of the higher civilization," [24] Eliot increased A.U.A. support in such college-center communities as Ann Arbor, Ithaca, Madison, and Berkeley.

Eliot used the power of organization to spread the Unitarian gospel. Having convened the first international congress of religious liberals in Boston in 1900, he turned to the domestic front, and in 1908 took the lead in forming the National Federation of Religious Liberals "to unify and concentrate the forces which make for religious sincerity, freedom, tolerance, and progress in America." [25] Wishing to exclude no one from the blessings of religious liberty, Eliot in 1909 invited unaffiliated liberals to become associate members of the Association, offering literature through the Post Office Mission and the assistance of a Unitarian minister if requested.

No stratagem escaped Eliot's notice. A portable church was constructed and used in Youngstown, Ohio.[26] A grant of $500 was voted in 1914 to the Unitarian churches in Philadelphia to counteract "the forthcoming visit of Billy Sunday to that city." [27] When All Souls Church in Washington, D.C. built its new church at 16th and Harvard streets, the A.U.A. awarded it a mortgage loan in the amount of $120,000 in return for its agreement that "the minister or ministers of All Souls Church shall be selected only with the approval of the Board of Directors of the American Unitarian Association." [28]

In response to an appeal from the White House to assist immigrants "as speedily as possible to shape themselves," the Association in 1905 established a committee on new Americans. The committee evolved into a full-fledged department, and by 1911 the A.U.A. was sponsoring eight workers among Icelandic, Swedish, Norwegian, Finnish, and Italian immigrants.[29] In 1913, a Unitarian mission church was gathered in Kingston, Jamaica, by the

Reverend Ethelred Brown, a graduate of Meadville Theological School.[30]

Eliot's early experiences in the Northwest and South inspired A.U.A. missionary efforts in behalf of native Americans and southern blacks. For decades the Association's budget included annual contributions to Hampton in Virginia, Tuskegee in Alabama, the Carolina Industrial School, the Palmer Memorial Institute, and other black institutions in South Carolina, Georgia, Florida, and Arkansas. In recognition of Eliot's commitment to the cause of native Americans, he was appointed in 1909 to the U. S. Board of Indian Commissioners by President William Howard Taft, a Unitarian. He took a keen interest in Indian affairs, visited reservations whenever his travel plans permitted, and advocated Indian self-government in Washington until President Franklin D. Roosevelt, soon after his first inauguration, abolished the board, of which Eliot had become chairman in 1927.[31]

One of Eliot's blind spots involved women in the ministry. In the years 1887 through 1897, no less than twenty-three women had received Unitarian ordination and two additional women transferred from other fellowships. In the sixteen years after 1901, in contrast, when Eliot was seeking to develop the untapped resources of the denomination, only one woman was ordained, the Reverend Rowena Morse at Geneva, Illinois, and one woman admitted from another fellowship. "The churches of Congregational polity," complained the Reverend Clara Cook Helvie, "are neglecting their woman power." [32]

III

The coming of war smashed the meliorist illusions of American Unitarians. In helpless horror they watched the European powers drift toward Armageddon. The Reverend Paul Revere Frothingham, minister of Boston's Arlington Street Church, told of his hairsbreadth escape from Germany in August, 1914, where he was attending an international peace conference in Constance. "The Kaiser and the Prussian war party may have wanted war," he wrote, "but there can be no doubt whatever of the peaceable inclinations of the German people. . . . The porter who took my bags at the railway station in Heidelberg turned away and burst into tears when I showed him the head-lines in the morning newspaper." [33] The *Register* saw in the guns of August "the prologue of what promises to be the greatest world-tragedy in history." [34]

The United States being a noncombatant nation, the American perspective in 1914 was that of sober disengagement. "They will best serve their generation," wrote the editor of the *Register*, "who are able to keep on the sunny side of life, and draw healing and strength from the permanent springs of virtue and blessedness." [35] A minister wrote: "The world will be more civilized, not less, after peace is won." [36]

A sense of comradeship with British Unitarians produced an appeal by the A.U.A. for support of the War Distress Fund launched to assist American and English tourists stranded on the continent and to provide clothing to the needy. In spite of President Wilson's appeal for nonpartisanship, many American Unitarians sided with England against the Central Powers, sharing the anguish of one British leader who wrote: "The entanglement of England in this fearful struggle is a bitter grief to those of us who have sought to cherish good will to Germany. . . . the suffering and loss entailed on so many, the combatants on both sides, . . . is an inexpressible sorrow." [37] The *Register* carried the full text of the German Appeal, a statement by the church historian Harnack on behalf of German pastors and theologians, asserting England's responsibility for the war, and the British reply.[38]

As the crisis deepened, Unitarian church school children sent contributions to Boston in behalf of the children of Belgium. The congregation of the First Parish Church of Scituate, "a small congregation of plain men and women," petitioned President Wilson to "appeal to the peoples now at war for an immediate cessation of hostilities." "We ourselves are suffering, and shall suffer, from this war," they declared. "Our accumulation of wealth which ought to finance a conquering war against disease, ignorance, poverty, vice, and crime in our own country must be heavily drawn upon to repair the ravages of the war in Europe." [39] In New York, John Haynes Holmes preached nine consecutive sermons on "Force vs. Non-resistance," adopting a pacifist position in which he was supported by his congregation.[40] In Winnipeg, the Reverend Horace Westwood urged: "The time to talk peace is *now*. . . . I would that every church society would form classes for the study of international polity and the preparation for peace. . . . Before the treaty!" [41]

The entrance of the United States in 1917 galvanized the full energies of the denomination in support of the war effort. A series of "war bulletins" was published urging the conservation of food and inviting donations to support religious work at mobilization camps.[42] A new pamphlet, "Twenty-Five Hymns for Use in Time of War," was distributed to service men.[43] The directors established a War Work Council under Eliot's chairmanship to coordinate the Association's support role.[44] "The officers and directors," proclaimed a Unitarian poster, "have adopted a policy of courage for the coming year." [45]

The conflict between those who supported the war and those who opposed it was explosively joined at the General Conference in September, 1917. Gathered in Montreal on the centennial of the peace treaty between the United States and Canada, the first such meeting to be held outside the United States, the delegates witnessed a frontal collision between the war power in the person of former President Taft, moderator of the General Conference, and the peace movement, as represented by John Haynes Holmes of New York, chairman of the council. "It is the duty of our church," exhorted Taft in his opening address,

> to preach the righteousness of the war and the necessity for our winning it in the interest of the peace of the world. . . . Let there be no doubt that our country's cause . . . is our cause. . . . I hope this Conference will by strong resolution express its emphatic approval of all that President Wilson and Congress have done and are doing to win this war.[46]

Acknowledging applause, Taft called on the chairman of the council to report. Settling into his chair, he heard the fiery Holmes denounce the war with stunning eloquence:

> This war . . . has driven men to the bowels of the earth, the depths of the sea, the vast spaces of the air, for combat. It has marshalled whole populations in the work of death. . . . Millions of men are dead on the battlefield or in the hospital, more millions are wounded,

maimed, blinded, or diseased, other millions including unnumbered women and children are . . . the nameless victims of famine, pestilence, and butchery. And still the fight goes on with a determination as wonderful as its cost is frightful.[47]

Sketching the representative attitudes of Unitarians toward the war—respectively those who would obliterate Germany, those who supported the war as the lesser of evils, those who sought to end the war at any price, and those who opposed war in principle —Holmes pleaded for "full, free, and fair statement of all points of view." [48] Holding that the war was "no flaming horror cast from another planet" but the creature of "our world" and "our breed," he saw the contest on the battlefield as "only the magnified reflection of the war of the factory, the slum, and the foreign market." [49] The council, he concluded, commends a ministry of reconciliation as the proper response of Unitarians to the war: "Hearts everywhere cry out for succor, hands grope for guidance, eyes stare in darkness for the light." [50]

Taft, enraged, yielded the chair and from the floor assailed Holmes's manifesto as "an insidious document." "Are we, as Unitarians, in favor of winning this war, or are we not?" he demanded, at length proposing a motion: "That it is the sense of this Unitarian Conference that this war must be carried to a successful issue, . . . that we . . . approve the measures of President Wilson and Congress to carry on this war . . ." [51]

In the debate, Holmes rose and said: "I am a pacifist, I am a non-resistant, I hate war, and I hate this war; so long as I live and breathe I will have nothing to do with this war or any war, so help me God." [52] Taft said: "Our house is afire and we must put it out, and it is no time for considering whether the firemen are using the best kind of water." [53] The motion was adopted by a vote of 236 to 9.[54]

In April, 1918, the directors of the A.U.A., concerned that certain ministers were causing discord in their parishes and in the denomination by continued opposition to the war, invoked sanctions. "The Association . . . reaffirms unreservedly its stand in support of the United States Government in the prosecution of the just and necessary war for freedom and humanity in which this nation is now engaged," the directors declared, adding that "any society which employs a minister who is not a willing, earnest, and outspoken supporter of the United States in the vigorous and resolute prosecution of the war cannot be considered eligible for aid from the Association." [55]

Holmes's response was to withdraw from the fellowship of Unitarian churches, and to launch a new movement of community churches.[56] The community church idea, coupled with the destruction of the Church of the Messiah by fire in 1919, occasioned Holmes's withdrawal from the A.U.A., but he acknowledged that the transformation was "a sign and symbol of the church's liberation . . . from its established denominational ties."

IV

The armistice in 1918 released the denomination's creative potential for reconstruction abroad and growth at home. Many Unitarians supported President Wilson's struggle for a League of Nations and his campaign for American ratification. "We are," said Eliot, "creating a new internationalism," adding that "in the war against war there can be no truce." [57]

The mistreatment of religious minorities in eastern Europe touched a raw nerve. The problem centered in Transylvania, the ancient Carpathian kingdom where Unitarianism had first emerged to history in the mid-sixteenth century. Under the Treaty of Versailles, Transylvania, historically a province of Hungary, was ceded to Romania. The Romanian government proceeded to deny basic liberties to the Transylvanians, regarding the country, according to one account, as a "conquered territory." [58] Confiscation of schools and churches, commandeering of dwellings, restrictions on the rights of public worship and public assembly were widespread.[59] A series of visitations, chiefly from English and American Unitarians, and the formation of an English and later an American Committee on Religious Rights and Minorities, served to call the world's attention to the conditions in Transylvania, and, in the words of one A.U.A. officer, helped to "stay the hand of ruthlessness and to give these minority institutions a better fighting chance for functioning and for surviving." [60] The Transylvanian movement did survive and maintains to this day in rural towns, some of them one-hundred per cent Unitarian, an invincible faith in the oneness of God and the perfectibility of humanity.

A further expression of international concern was the effort to establish a Unitarian movement in Czechoslovakia. With the creation in 1918 of the Republic of Czechoslovakia out of the old Austro-Hungarian kingdoms of Bohemia, Moravia, Silesia, and Slovakia, more than a million Roman Catholics left the Church. Seeking an indigenous church home, they formed the Czechoslovak Church, often misnamed the "national church," which was episcopal in polity and orthodox in liturgy but liberal in theology. Through the International Council and its member churches a friendly hand was extended to the Czechoslovak Church. One expression of this friendship was the conferring of the honorary degree of Doctor of Divinity on Patriarch Prochaska by the Meadville Theological School at a special convocation in Prague in 1934. In addition, by virtue of the loyalty to Unitarianism of the wife of the president of the Czechoslovak Republic, Charlotte Garrigue Masaryk, efforts were begun to establish an avowedly Unitarian church in the Bohemian capital. In 1921, the Reverend and Mrs. Norbert Capek were sent to Prague for that purpose. Starting from scratch, the Capeks succeeded in forming the largest Unitarian congregation in the world, numbering 3,395 in 1932.[61] Norbert Capek was murdered by the Nazis at Dachau in November, 1942;[62] his widow resided in California until her death in 1966.

A third manifestation of post-war internationalism was the rapprochement between American and Filipino religious liberals. In 1928, a chance remark brought to the attention of American Unitarian leaders the Independent Church of the Philippines, formed in 1905 by the withdrawal of several million persons from the Roman Catholic church at the time of Spain's defeat in the Spanish American War and the consequent cession of the islands to the United States. A liaison of approximately a decade led certain leaders of the American movement to hope that the Independent Church would become Unitarian. Louis C. Cornish of Boston was made honorary president of the Independent Church, an office previously held by William Howard Taft when American commissioner to the Philippines prior to his election as president.[63] But the Independent Church, which Cornish described as "nothing less than the Philippine Protestant Reformation long delayed by Spanish tyranny," [64] finally elected to affiliate with the Episcopal rather than the Unitarian churches, the Anglican liturgy and doctrine being more consonant with the new communion's Catholic antecedents.[65]

At home, the Unitarians exploited the ending of hostilities for denominational purposes, as Bellows had in 1865. A Unitarian campaign in 1922 raised more than two million dollars. The A.U.A. considered establishing a Unitarian radio station, but nothing came of the plan.[66] The Unitarian Laymen's League, formed in 1907 to establish lay centers in communities where no Unitarian church existed, in 1919 turned its energies to publicizing the Unitarian cause.[67] Within five years the League had 270 chapters and 12,000 members, with offices and agents in four cities.[68] Unitarian rallies were held throughout the country, addressed by mission preachers sponsored by the League. In 1927, the Reverend Horace Westwood resigned the pulpit of the church in Toledo to become staff mission preacher. Prominent ministers undertook speaking tours to unchurched cities and to college campuses under the Billings lectureship fund.[69] President Eliot visited scores of churches annually, and his salary appeared in the A.U.A. budget under the category: "general missionary work." [70] Eliot thought it "no overwhelming task" for the president to know, as he himself knew, "every man on the list of ministers and the condition and prospects of every church." [71]

Unitarianism grew by adding on, by spinning off. In 1924, St. John's Church in Cincinnati, a liberal Protestant congregation consisting largely of German immigrants, affiliated with the A.U.A., as did the Independent Protestant Church of Columbus, Ohio, three years later.[72] In contrast, the Unitarian missionary to Japan, the Reverend John B. W. Day, recommended that responsibility for Unitarian work in Japan be transferred to the Japanese themselves, and that he should return to America, which he did.[73]

A major reorganization of the A.U.A. occurred in 1925. The General Conference, established as the National Conference sixty years before, was integrated into the Association, but the mechanism of biennial conference meetings was retained in order to enable Unitarians to meet away from Boston, where the regular annual business meeting continued to be held. In addition, the term of office of the president was extended, and Eliot was elected to a four-year term. A commission on survey appointed in 1925, while reporting its general satisfaction with the state of the denomination, recommended that "the courses in ministerial preparation" at Unitarian theological schools should "be built rather about the social sciences than about the topics [i.e., theology, Bible, church history] which have hitherto formed the nucleus of the classical discipline in divinity schools." [74]

Most Unitarian ministers were trained at one of three centers, the Harvard Divinity School in Massachusetts, the Meadville Theological School in Pennsylvania, and the Pacific Unitarian School in California. An arrangement of affiliation between Harvard and the Andover Theological Seminary, a Congregational institution, undertaken in 1908 as a measure both of reconciliation and of increased efficiency, was voided by the courts in 1926. Andover professors, it was determined, were still bound by the ancient Andover Creed, with its condemnation of Unitarian errors. The schools went their separate ways except in the matter of library resources. [75]

Founded in northwest Pennsylvania in 1844, Meadville was essentially a regional institution serving the western churches in the same manner in which Harvard served the New England churches, until late in the century, when the schools gradually achieved parity. Although not requiring an undergraduate degree for admission, Meadville maintained high academic standards and pioneered in the education of women ministers. Responding to the shift in higher education from a collegiate to a university model, and to the advancing urbanization of nation and denomination, Meadville instituted a "Chicago semester" in 1906, and finally, in 1926, relocated its faculty, students, and instructional program in that city in affiliation with the University of Chicago. [76]

The Pacific School developed in response to a demand by West Coast Unitarians for an institution independent of Boston and sensitive to regional needs. As early as 1887, Samuel Eliot recognized the desirability of a western school, [77] and he encouraged it during his years of denominational leadership. The school was launched in the Bay Area in 1905 with the Reverend Earl Morse Wilbur as president. [78] Called from a ministry in Meadville, Penn-

sylvania, Wilbur served as the A.U.A.'s West Coast field representative during the first years of his presidency, shaping the
school in close linkage with the ministers and churches for which
he was responsible. Several factors, including the A.U.A.'s central
role in its founding, its distance from Boston, and its lack of
capital resources, have contributed to the Pacific school's depen-
dence on direct A.U.A. support. Its first building, containing a
library, faculty offices, and a chapel, was financed by a grant of
$45,000 from the Unitarian campaign of 1922.[79] It was from his
presidency at Berkeley that Dr. Wilbur embarked upon his
massive and original researches into the history of Unitarianism,
culminating in his two-volume masterpiece, *A History of Unitarianism*, completed in 1952.[80]

V

The predominant theological position within Unitarianism in
the early years of the century was what Samuel Eliot called
"lyrical theism." [81] It affirmed an ordered universe governed by a
benign deity who acted through nature, law, and spirit upon the
souls of men, and who responded to prayer and good works with
a hastened sense of cosmic realization. "Our best tool for building
the Kingdom of God," rhapsodized a Unitarian official in 1903,
"is a Unitarian church." [82] Individual ministers brought their
special accents to the theological task, including Minot Savage's
excursions into spiritualism, Richard Boynton's studies of modernism, and Newton Mann's ponderings on evolution, each con-
tributing to a wide consensus on faith and worship which was
undergirded rather than threatened by Darwinism and by German
scholarship. "Science is but attempting to think God's thoughts
after Him," a minister declared in 1927.[83]

Dean Charles Carroll Everett's application of Hegelian theory
to Christian theology, and Francis Greenwood Peabody's inductive
research in ethics and social pathology, both centered at Harvard,
influenced the Unitarian theological consensus through the nur-
ture of ministers and in books and articles. Building on the axioms
of Emerson and Parker, and latterly of William James and John

Dewey, the leaders of Unitarian thought in the early decades of the century held experience to be the key alike to knowledge, devotion, and social reconstruction. The social matrix of individual salvation was widely assumed, as in Holmes's assertion that the individual is a social creature and "must be reached, if . . . at all, through the conditions of the social environment." [84] Christian in symbolism, Romantic in spirit, inclusive in sympathy, Unitarian Christianity—its foundations shaken but not toppled by world war—trusted the future and did not doubt the ultimate triumph of good over evil. Eliot's catechism for the churches, prepared for Association Day in 1907, catches the Unitarian consensus. The minister asks: "What is the faith of our Unitarian churches?" The people reply, in the words of the Saratoga Conference (1894): "These churches affirm the religion of Jesus, holding, in accordance with his teaching, that practical religion is summed up in love to God and love to man." Minister: "Why should we spread this gospel?" People: "To do our part in bringing in the Kingdom of God and to make truth and righteousness the foundation of the nation." [85]

An influential voice of Unitarian Christianity was that of William Laurence Sullivan, a convert from Catholicism. Born in Braintree, Massachusetts, in 1872, the son of Irish immigrants, Sullivan was ordained a Paulist priest in 1899. As preacher, teacher, and propagandist, he rose quickly in Roman Catholic circles and gave promise of a large career. A classicist, he read widely in a number of languages.[86]

It was Sullivan's misfortune that the Church of Rome rejected modernism at the very moment he, in the company of other progressive Catholics, was embracing it. Although fully orthodox at ordination, he soon found himself forced to choose between spiritual freedom and what he felt to be ecclesiastical tyranny. Condemning Inquisition as sanctified murder, he himself became the victim of a witchhunt in the modernist struggle.

The crisis peaked in 1907 when Pope Pius X issued a decree, *Lamentabili*, and an encyclical, *Pascendi*, condemning all aspects of modernism and commanding extreme measures to purge the church. In 1910, all Catholic priests and teachers were ordered to subscribe, in the anti-modernist oath, to a personal repudiation of modern science, democracy, and biblical criticism, under threat of excommunication.[87] For Sullivan this was the ultimate humiliation. In the company of Alfred Loisy and other modernist spokesmen, he left the church rather than compromise his fidelity to conscience and to Christ. "I discovered," he wrote later, "that the whole orbit of my mind was set in a different space and round another center." [88]

Sullivan's pilgrimage finally led him to marriage and to Unitarianism, where he found a home, a career, and an audience. In 1914, two years after his break with Rome, he addressed a grievance to the Pope, entitled *Letters to His Holiness Pope Pius X*, in which he asserted the principles of liberty, condemned Vatican barbarism, and advocated the separation of Church and State. Describing the torture of heretics as "the lowest infamy ever reached by man," he advocated salvation by character and called on the Pope to live "the Christ-life." [89] As minister in Schenectady, New York, New York City (All Souls), St. Louis, and at the Germantown congregation in Philadelphia, also as mission preacher of the Unitarian Laymen's League, he preached effortlessly without notes, drawing on his struggles in the modernist crisis to illumine the true nature of reformed Christianity. He died in 1935.

A number of theological movements arose in counterpoint to liberal Christianity, including the neo-orthodox assertion of the finality of Christ, identified with Karl Barth in Europe and with Reinhold Niebuhr in the United States; and the process school based on the thought of Alfred North Whitehead, identified with Henry Nelson Wieman at the University of Chicago. One such movement was distinctively Unitarian. This was the movement of religious humanism.

Humanism placed man at the center and regarded God as at best a model of creation, at worst a monstrous delusion. An early spokesman defined humanism as "faith in the supreme value and self-perfectibility of human personality," [90] a rubric which would cover most of the religious humanists. Like their spiritual forebears in sixteenth-century Europe, the humanists emerged one by one on the religious landscape, isolated radicals in voluntary exile from supernatural theology and churchly intolerance, each pursuing a one-man reformation under the aegis of Unitarianism.

John H. Dietrich of Pittsburgh, expelled in 1911 from the ministry of the Reformed Church for defiance of the Heidelberg Catechism, became minister of the Unitarian church of Spokane, Washington.[91] Charles Francis Potter, maverick minister of a Baptist church in Mattapan, Massachusetts, resigned in 1914—"I can't sail under false colors," he announced at the time—to take up a ministry at the Unitarian church in Edmonton, Alberta.[92] Curtis W. Reese, a graduate of Southern Baptist Seminary in Louisville, his orthodoxy eroded by biblical criticism, in 1913 became minister of the Unitarian church in Alton, Illinois.[93] Reconstructing their religious faith in resonance with Theodore Parker and the western liberals, the religious humanists gradually made contact with each other. Unitarian humanism was born.

The impulse toward non-theistic, non-Christian Unitarianism was hardly new. It was anticipated by some of the members of the Free Religious Association, and in some measure in the western movement of which the Reverend Jenkin Lloyd Jones of Chicago, editor of *Unity*, was representative. The controversy over the Christian or "ethical" basis of Unitarianism, pursued at New York in 1865, in Cincinnati in 1886, and at Saratoga in 1894, resulted in the diffusion of "ethical" principles, thereby preparing the ground for humanism. In addition, what amounted to a reconciliation of the A.U.A. with the Western Unitarian Conference at Saratoga in 1894 had the effect of extending the ethical position beyond its regional base, legitimating it as a national movement.[94]

The humanist movement gained momentum as its leaders found their audience and entered positions of denominational influence: Dietrich at the First Unitarian Church of Minneapolis; Potter at the West Side Unitarian church in New York City; Reese in the Des Moines pulpit, and then, in 1919, in Chicago as secretary of the Western Unitarian Conference. Enflamed by sermons, tracts, books, resolutions, letters to the editor, and the debates between Dietrich and Sullivan, and between Potter and John R. Straton, humanism swept through the denomination, becoming its most vital and distinctive theological movement since Transcendentalism. Advocating science against supernaturalism, democracy against tyranny, reason against superstition, experience against revelation, humanists plowed new ground among the Unitarians,

Samuel Atkins Eliot

John Haynes Holmes

Earl Morse Wilbur

Louis Craig Cornish

Egbert Ethelred Brown

eventually achieving parity in numbers and influence with the liberal Christian position. Some ministers, such as Holmes, embraced elements both of Christianity and of humanism and declined to commit themselves to the new movement to the exclusion of long-standing loyalties. Others, such as Frederick M. Eliot of St. Paul, participated selectively, joining forces with the humanists on some issues but opposing them on others. Still others, such as Richard Boynton of Buffalo, while welcoming the critical power of humanism in relation to ideas and institutions, rejected the humanists' anthropocentrism as "pre-Copernican."

As often happens, the definitive statement of humanist principles came when the movement had begun to lose its innovative spirit. In the winter and spring of 1932-33, inspired by the New Deal and appalled at the rise of fascism in Europe, a group of Chicago humanists decided to compress humanist ideals into a public statement. They invited Roy Wood Sellars, professor of philosophy at the University of Michigan, to prepare a draft. Sellars did so, offering a series of theses in the manner of Luther's argument against indulgences. The draft statement circulated among a large constituency, some signing, others offering amendments, others refusing. Holmes, although close to the Chicago humanists as editor of *Unity*, declined, charging that the sixth article, which proscribed "theism, deism, modernism, and the several varieties of 'new thought,'" excluded "from our thought something about which you know absolutely nothing at all." Professor Max Otto at Wisconsin disparaged the statement as "one of those theoretical gestures which leave with some persons a feeling that something has been done when all that has been done is that something has been said." [95]

The Humanist Manifesto was published in *The New Humanist* in May-June, 1933. There is, it asserts, danger of a final identification of the word "religion" with "doctrines and methods which have lost their significance and which are powerless to solve the problem of human living in the Twentieth Century." Hence any religion "that can hope to be a synthesizing and dynamic force for today must be shaped for the needs of this age." The Manifesto asserts the universe to be "self-existing and not created," denies "supernatural or cosmic guarantees of human values," and affirms that "nothing human is alien to the religious." The goal of humanism, it holds, "is a free and universal society in which people voluntarily and intelligently coöperate for the common good. Humanists demand a shared life in a shared world." [96]

Thirty-four persons, including John Dewey, signed the Humanist Manifesto, all of them men and half of them Unitarian and Universalist ministers. Although it caused a sensation in some circles, the Manifesto appeared in the *Register* without comment. The Reverend Lon Ray Call, himself a humanist, remarked three months after its publication that the Manifesto "fell like a dud in the battle-scarred career of American theological thought." [97]

VI

Prosperity buoyed the Unitarians. Church budgets climbed, ministerial salaries soared, and the Association spent $170,000 in 1927, the largest budgeted amount in its history. The war receded in memory, and in spite of Wilson's failure, Unitarians continued to agitate for American entry into the League and the World Court. New church buildings were dedicated during 1927, in Germantown, Salt Lake City, and Los Angeles. In Boston the A.U.A. building on Beacon Street at the corner of Bowdoin had been sold to the Bellevue Hotel for its expansion, and a new headquarters was erected two hundred yards to the west, on the other side of the State House. In recognition of the role of women in the churches, Mrs. Oscar Gallagher of Brookline, president of the Alliance of Unitarian Women, turned the first shovelful of earth in the construction. The number "25" moved with the new headquarters by vote of the General Court.

In May, 1927, Samuel Eliot resigned the presidency to accept the pulpit of Boston's Arlington Street Church. Thirty-five years earlier, when, as minister in Denver, he was being considered for the Arlington Street post, a member of the latter congregation objected to his youth, saying: "What this church needs is roast beef, not calves' brains." [98] Now the church had roast beef.

Eliot had led the A.U.A. as director, secretary, and president, for thirty-three years, almost one-third of its existence. Only once, in 1912, had his leadership been seriously challenged. A group led by John Haynes Holmes opposed his reëlection on the ground that the A.U.A. had become a business organization and had ceased to be a spiritual force. Although not yet fifty at the time, Eliot was portrayed as a traditionalist whose methods thwarted the development of a new Unitarianism in process of birth. Eliot turned back the challenge, winning office by a vote of 637 to 67.[99]

The achievements of the Eliot administration were impressive. The Association's endowments had increased twelvefold, from half a million to six million dollars. The staff had grown from four to twenty-five persons. The church building loan fund had granted almost 300 loans to churches without losing a dollar.[100] The strategy of investment of bequests, collective investment of designated funds, and a pay-as-you-go budget system was proven. Reviewing his years of leadership, Eliot remarked: "Twenty-five years ago the weak spot of our denomination . . . was in the center. This Association was feeble and incompetent. We needed a strong center if we were to amount to anything. It is strong today, and we are weak not at the center but at the circumference. The weak spot now is in our parish churches." [101]

What prompted Eliot to resign midway through his term of office? His father had died the year before, having retired from the presidency of Harvard in 1909. The Association had celebrated its centennial and stabilized its finances and management. A new headquarters building was in place. Eliot was sixty-four. The decisive factor, however, may have been the call to the active parish ministry. Eliot had relinquished the ministry reluctantly in 1898. He had never stopped preaching. He enjoyed good health. An invitation from the "cathedral church" of Unitarianism, which he hoped to restore to its former glory as a metropolitan center of liberal religion for city and suburbs alike, proved irresistible. The fact that the church encouraged him to continue his work in Indian affairs, prison reform, world peace, soil conservation, and Unitarian biography was an additional inducement.[102]

Eliot thought of himself as a Christian and a fighter. Married in 1889 to Frances Hopkinson, niece of his father's second wife, he thrived on the family's intimate and boisterous life at home, as his seven children grew, departed, and returned with grandchildren for him to love. His life spanned the years from Abraham

Lincoln to Mao Tse-Tung, from slavery to F.E.P.C., from horse-drawn carriages to jet power. "Out of a multiplicity of independent, self-engrossed congregations and lay people," his biographer has written, "he brought into being a self-conscious coöperative enterprise, with a sense of its own identity and purpose, the Unitarian denomination." [103] Eliot was the best embodiment of his own principle that "when you get to the heart of religion you find it a marching song." [104] He died in 1950.

Who would succeed him? The fact that he resigned in mid-term required that the board of directors name a successor. In June, 1927, the board named Louis Craig Cornish as president for eight months, until a new election could be held at the next annual meeting.

Cornish was a native of New Bedford, the son of a physician. Educated at Stanford and Harvard, he was ordained at King's Chapel in 1899. After a period as secretary to Bishop William Lawrence of the Episcopal diocese of Massachusetts, he was called in 1900 to the pulpit of the Old Ship Church in Hingham, on the South Shore. He served for fifteen years, which included a stint as volunteer librarian at A.U.A. headquarters. He was named the Association's secretary-at-large, a full-time position, in 1915, and secretary of the board of directors the following year. In 1925, he was promoted to administrative vice president, the office from which he entered the presidency.[105]

Cornish was chosen by a vote of ten to four.[106] The *Register* welcomed his appointment as "the wisest thing for the steady continuance of our united church labors. We shall go right forward without the least sense of interruption." [107]

The new president, for his part, cautioned the denomination not to reach beyond its grasp. Mindful of the Unitarian Foundation campaign of 1925, in which less than a third of the two-million-dollar goal was achieved, Cornish in his first major address as president announced a policy of retrenchment. "I plead that during these next eight months we cease to try to get on too quickly, and that we drop the line of our desires." He proposed an annual increase in membership and contributions of "at least five per cent," noting that "if we can do this every year, in about seventeen years we shall double" our resources. "I submit," he argued, "that the lower line of planning is the line on which we ought to proceed during this coming year." [108] Eliot, speaking at the same meeting, cited the tenfold increase in A.U.A. income during his period of leadership, and suggested the motto: *"L'audace—toujours l'audace!"* [109]

Uncertain of his support in the ranks, Cornish surveyed the Unitarian ministers to assess sentiment respecting his presidency. Of 518 surveyed, 307 responded. Of these 237 preferred a minister as president, 32 preferred a layman, and 38 either indicated no choice or left the question blank. Cornish himself was preferred for the office by 166 respondents, if first and second choices are combined, which placed him far ahead of the others named, all of whom were ministers of major churches or regional executives. [110]

Cornish was most interested in visiting churches and cultivating international contacts. He was not trained in administration, nor did his experience in the ministry prepare him for high responsibility. His effort to secure the liberties of religious liberals in eastern Europe was an outstanding achievement, chronicled in two books, *Transylvania in 1922* (1923) and *The Religious Minorities of Transylvania* (1925). He travelled throughout the continent and the world in behalf of the Unitarian cause; and whereas Eliot's correspondence to the *Register* consisted of hard-nosed commentary on the state of the churches, Cornish inclined to a travelogue style, in which scenery, architecture, and audience statistics predominated.

The Association was not without accomplishment in Cornish's first year. The directors authorized a hymnal commission to update the *Hymn and Tune Book*, the denomination's hymnal published in 1914 which was distinguished by a format that placed the words of each hymn at the bottom of the page. [111] When the Universalists appointed a similar commission, the two groups joined forces and in 1937 created *Hymns of the Spirit*.

An administrative council was formalized in 1928, confirming existing practice. The council consisted of the three major officers plus four other directors. Convened fortnightly by the president, it had "general superintendence of all the operations of the Association" and executed all matters authorized by the board of directors. [112] In practice the council soon replaced the board as the decision-making arm of the denomination, a development which removed policy a further step away from the churches and tended to isolate the officers without their being aware of it. It was symptomatic of Cornish's administrative style, as former secretary and vice president, that the Association's display advertisement in the *Register* read: "Address all communications to Dr. Louis C. Cornish." [113]

VII

Already weakened by a change in leadership, the denomination was further enfeebled by the advent of the Depression. Many churches lost heavily in the stock market, although one, at least, the Community Church of New York, having much of its capital invested in real estate, survived relatively unscathed. The A.U.A.'s income from investments plummeted, forcing heavy cutbacks in salaries, travel, and aid to churches. As trustee of scores of church-owned endowments, the Association was able to maintain a financial floor for many constituent societies which might otherwise have been wiped out by the crash.

A ten per cent salary cut for senior officers was voted.[114] The Toledo church, its new building heavily mortgaged, was bailed out when the Association purchased the first mortgage for $40,000, then borrowed a like sum from a Boston bank on a demand note.[115] As a concession to churches in arrears to the building loan fund, the directors instructed the treasurer "not to resort to legal measures to collect payment of principal or interest now overdue . . . unless otherwise instructed." [116] The board declined a request to guarantee credit to Proctor Academy in Andover, New Hampshire, but voted a special appropriation to the Pacific Unitarian School to save it from bankruptcy. The biennial conference in 1933 was omitted, and the directors chose to meet bimonthly rather than monthly. Contributions from the churches dropped from $50,000 to $30,000 in 1933, and a budget cut of $80,000 in that year was required.[117]

From Minnesota a voice was heard advocating planning as a central function of the new society. The Reverend Frederick M. Eliot wrote in the *Register* that it "makes very little difference whether the planned order be based upon the philosophy of Karl Marx and Lenin or upon . . . American individualism, for the responsibility for planning will rest upon a comparatively few persons and in either case the results will be decisively affected by the way in which those few have been educated." [118] Eliot urged the denomination to strengthen its planning capability both at headquarters and in the field.

In spite of demoralization, or perhaps because of it, the A.U.A. attempted to extend the denomination's outreach to unchurched areas. The directors voted to survey United States cities of 100,000 population or more where "it is desirable to establish Unitarian churches when funds are available." [119] The administrative council formulated plans for starting five new churches, and in 1931, Cornish announced that the Association hoped to establish societies in Asheville, North Carolina; Savannah; Phoenix; and South Bend; but none materialized.[120]

The history of the denomination in these years is strewn with missed opportunities. In Harlem, the Reverend Ethelred Brown, twenty years earlier the leader of a mission church in Jamaica, British West Indies, started the Harlem Unitarian church, but it languished.[121] Another experiment was the Bronx Free Fellowship, a congregation of blue collar workers and their families led by the Reverend Leon R. Land with support from the New York regional office.[122] This was the first Unitarian congregation to avail itself of the educational genius of Mrs. Sophia Lyon Fahs of Union Theological Seminary, who at the fellowship's request prepared a new church school curriculum. Unfortunately, no copy has survived.[123] In 1933, the A.U.A. voted a study of Unitarian city churches to identify factors which "make up a successful and effective church, and the opportunities of such churches for social usefulness." [124] After eight months, upon recommendation of the administrative council, the directors voted that "the proposed survey of downtown churches . . . be indefinitely postponed." [125]

What was the A.U.A. doing during these years? Basically it was continuing the priorities and procedures of the Eliot administration, but with diminished resources, limited imagination, and an administrative structure that strangled new ideas. A case in point is the Association's effort to salvage Lombard College. Lombard was established by Universalists in Galesburg, Illinois. Never distinguished, it foundered in the economic unrest following the war, and in 1928 its trustees approached the A.U.A. for help. It was arranged that in return for the assignment to the college of the income from $250,000 of the Association's capital, the A.U.A. would name the president and a majority of trustees. Curtis W. Reese, secretary of the Western Unitarian Conference and a leading humanist, was named president. But a capital fund drive undertaken in 1930 was unsuccessful, the crash having intervened, and the arrangement collapsed. The residual assets of Lombard College passed to the Meadville Theological School. In this episode, in pursuit of Eliot's commitment to Unitarian-sponsored nonsectarian education, Cornish sought to strengthen a needy institution under the coöperative auspices of Unitarians and Universalists, but the times were unpropitious and the experiment turned to ashes.[126]

The denomination's work in religious education repeated the pattern. A new department of religious education having been established in 1912, and an ambitious graded curriculum, the Beacon Course, having been underwritten with funds from the Unitarian Sunday School Society, the Association failed during the 1920s to maintain its initiative in work with children. The Boston leadership was unresponsive to the revolutionary developments in education flowing from John Dewey and others. The most conspicuous failure lay in not utilizing Mrs. Fahs of New York, who, although involved with Unitarians in the middle Atlantic region, was for the most part ignored by headquarters until a new departmental officer, Ernest W. Kuebler, secured her appointment as children's editor later in the decade.[127]

Cornish excelled in international diplomacy. He travelled to distant congresses, there to mingle with representatives of other world religions. He loved the international protocol of robed processions, honorary degrees, and engrossed resolutions of greeting, never failing to inform the directors of an anniversary in Hungary or Japan. In 1934, he announced that the International Association with headquarters in The Hague embraced "a total membership exceeding twenty million people." [128] But his support was fragile, his constituents restless. That same year in a letter to the *Register* he felt obliged to defend the decision of the directors to pay his expenses as A.U.A. delegate to an international meeting in Denmark.[129]

A kindred impulse was the effort to bring Unitarians and Universalists together. In 1899, Eliot had initiated a rapprochement which foundered when the joint committee, responding to Universalist pressure, announced: "We seek coöperation, not consolidation; unity, not union." [130] Undaunted, Eliot convened an international congress in Boston in 1900. Underlying his larger intention was the hope, as he expressed it, of reacting "upon our own churches at home" in behalf of church unity.[131] Relations continued cordial but desultory until 1927. On learning that the Universalists had been negotiating privately with the National Council of Congregational Churches, Eliot admonished them. "When . . . you have got through making polite bows to orthodoxy," he wrote, "then the Unitarians will be glad to welcome you back to the glorious toils and perils of the pioneers—only we have been steadily on the march, and you may have to run a little to catch up." [132] Abandoning their flirtation with the Congregationalists, the Universalists agreed to joint fellowship for Unitarian and Universalist ministers (sixty-five responded),[133] a denomination-wide pulpit exchange,[134] and a joint hymnal.

A distinctive expression of Unitarian and Universalist coöperation in the 1930s was the Free Church of America, later called the Free Church Fellowship. Hoping to effect "the final union of the forces of liberal religion" in America,[135] Cornish and others envisioned a federation of liberal religious denominations, societies, and individuals, which would be governed by a council resembling the A.U.A.'s administrative council. Cornish was elected president. "This is the day of the Lord," exulted the Reverend George E. Huntley in October, 1933, when the Universalists voted to affiliate. "I have prayed night and day for this hour. I dare use the great name Pentecost to describe it." [136] Others were less sanguine. "What has become of the Free Church Fellowship?" asked Holmes in the *Register*, a year later. "Is it dead, deceased, dying, defunct, dormant, or just plain discouraged?" [137]

In fact, the Fellowship never became a popular movement. It attracted a Congregationalist or two and a Methodist bishop, but it had no broad support beyond the Unitarian and Universalist communities. The Fellowship was plagued by misfortune from the beginning, its first annual meeting being held in Brooklyn during the worst snow storm in fifty years.[138] After three years its epitaph was written when the A.U.A. directors voted, in spite of Cornish's pleadings, to make no appropriation for its work.[139]

In the realm of social responsibility, a department of social relations had been formed in 1927 with Robert C. Dexter, Professor of Social and Political Science at Skidmore College, as executive secretary.[140] Early in the century, a department of social and public service had been established by Eliot, later known as the department of community service.[141] It is possible that this initial action was Eliot's response to the organization in 1908 by Holmes and others of the Unitarian Fellowship for Social Justice, an independent agency "for united action against all forms of social injustice."

Dexter was an experienced catalyst of social change in both theory and practice. When the mill workers of Marion, North Carolina, went on strike in 1930, he solicited money and clothing for their families.[142] His on-site analysis of the cotton industry in New England, then in flight to the cheap labor markets of the South, was published and distributed by the A.U.A.[143]

Dexter's activities, in which he was supported by Roy M. Cushman of the Boston Council of Social Agencies, who served as chairman of the A.U.A.'s departmental committee, predictably provoked the wrath of conservative elements in the denomination. When in 1930 it was proposed that the department be terminated, Dexter's hand was strengthened by a survey of representative ministers and laymen in which sixty of sixty-one respondents urged that the work go forward.[144]

In an effort to unleash Dexter from the constraints of the conservatives on the board, his supporters persuaded the 1934 A.U.A. annual meeting to authorize the department of social relations to speak independently of the Association. The result was the "program of social action," a landmark statement of social goals and strategies published in February, 1935. The program called for nationalization of arms manufacture, abandonment of violence both by employers and by employees, and "government control and ownership of public utilities, transportation, banking, coal, and other natural resources." It also advocated equal opportunity for women, and support of the League, World Court, and anti-lynching laws.[145] Although far from radical in an era of Norman

Clara Cook Helvie (1876-1958) was the only woman minister to participate in the dedicatory service of the new headquarters building in 1927. Interested in the careers of women ministers, she compiled biographies of both Unitarian and Universalist women ministers.

Thomas and Franklin D. Roosevelt, the program, which was publicized in the press before the *Register* could print it, provoked both praise and outrage. A member of the A.U.A. Board resigned when his effort to muzzle the department failed.[146]

As the A.U.A.'s state of depression deepened, with churches closing and growing numbers of ministers unemployed or forced to take second jobs, the senior officers and directors were lulled by a series of internal audits. In 1929, a committee on comparative values consisting of five directors made "no adverse criticism," holding that "the main emphasis is put where it belongs." [147] In 1932, a commission on survey examined the policies of the Association but made no substantive criticisms.[148] To a demand by the Unitarian Ministerial Union in 1933 for a "recovery program" to restore salaries and strengthen the churches, Cornish replied that in spite of reductions in denominational income the morale of the churches was "high." [149]

In May, 1934, the storm broke. Building on the discontent of the ministers, and recalling the work of the appraisal group that had conducted the Laymen's Foreign Missions Inquiry, Kenneth McDougall, a layman in the Wellesley Hills church, stated the case against the A.U.A. leadership. "Neither today nor for several years past have we . . . had a program worthy of our traditions and opportunities," he wrote.

> We drift, we play with such naive notions as "putting 100,000 Unitarians to work," we . . . contemplate a happy future with annual increases of five per cent. We content ourselves with exchanging good will with a group of liberal Filipinos. . . . We are known less and less as a pioneering and prophetic church.

Citing the "inbreeding" that led to Cornish's selection as president of the Free Church Fellowship and as A.U.A. delegate to Copenhagen, McDougall uttered the fateful words: "Let there be for the Association a commission of appraisal." [150]

As the denomination, impotent to harness its own best energies, groped for a future, across the Atlantic, fascism gathered momentum toward its goal of racial mastery in Europe. Were the two situations related? "The only way to help stricken Germans," pleaded John Haynes Holmes in January, 1934, "is to get them out of Germany while there is time." [151] Meanwhile in the board room of the American Unitarian Association Louis Cornish presented a request from the American Civil Liberties Union that the Association petition President Roosevelt to allow more immigrants to enter the country from Germany. The minutes record: "No action was taken." [152]

Chapter 5

"It Was Noontime Here..."

Frederick May Eliot and
the Unitarian Renaissance, 1934-1961

I

The world in 1934 was still recoiling from depression; Adolf Hitler had been in power for a year, an awesome shadow cast on the horizon; and in just a few years the human family was to be rent asunder in the horror of another war. On religious structures in the United States, economic instability and philosophical anxieties had made their impact. The religious body was in ill health.

Unitarians were not exempt. Unitarian churches were in sharp decline, and some people even feared that Unitarianism might die as an institution. Dr. Louis C. Cornish, president of the American Unitarian Association, painted a dismal picture of the situation:

Churches are being consolidated; churches are being closed. One Protestant denomination reports 500 unemployed ministers in New England alone. There is no need of amplifying these statements. There is need to remember that the present day conditions affect every coöperative endeavor, including the work of the American Unitarian Association. It has been impossible for this Association to do all we would wish it to do.[1]

Out of a sense of concern for the future of Unitarianism comparable to that felt in 1865 by an earlier generation, there came a call for reassessment and a new beginning. In the spring of 1934 at the Unitarian Society of Wellesley Hills, Massachusetts, where James Luther Adams was minister, there were bull sessions in which the Unitarian bureaucracy was sharply criticized. Dr. Adams has referred to them as "gripe sessions." [2] As a result the suggestion was made in emphatic terms: "What we need is an Appraisal Commission!"

Prominent in these discussions was Kenneth McDougall, head of the Laymen's League chapter at the Wellesley church. Adams and he secured money for expenses from a member of the church, and barnstormed up and down the East Coast, urging action at the coming May Meetings of the A.U.A. Wide support was elicited, and even before the resolution they proposed was presented to the delegates at the business meeting, a dozen or more persons were prepared with speeches in favor.

So it was that on May 22, 1934, the Reverend Frank O. Holmes, chairman of the Committee on Resolutions, offered the following:

WHEREAS: The recent action of the Essex Unitarian Conference calling for the devotion "of all the available resources of man power, organization and finance to an advance movement throughout the entire fellowship," and a second resolution adopted by the Unitarian Ministerial Union urging upon the administration of the American Unitarian Association a definite effort to establish a Recovery Program, have given evidence of widespread unrest regarding the future of the Unitarian movement, and have made articulate the prevalent sense of imperative need for a reappraisal of values and a reconsideration of methods.

BE IT RESOLVED: By the American Unitarian Association in annual meeting assembled.

(1) That a Commission of Appraisal be immediately appointed to survey our work both in theory and practice.

To appraise the methods now in use, and

To recommend clarification of principles and changes in policy, program, and organization, wherever and however they may be necessary. [3]

The resolution continued with five more stipulations and was passed unanimously.

The concern expressed in the resolution did not derive from any widespread belief that the administration was corrupt or grossly negligent. Rather, it was felt that in any bureaucratic set-up, dissatisfactions will arise, especially if the bureaucracy has been in power for a long time. There was a general feeling among

Unitarians that the situation was desperate. New methods, new leadership might help in building up the institution. New directions might be based on the insights that would come from a systematic and thorough appraisal of the status and goals of collective Unitarianism. The proposal was a reaction to the fact that Unitarianism was not growing and thriving, at least partly as a result of socio-economic conditions, and was not a personal attack on Dr. Samuel A. Eliot and Dr. Louis C. Cornish, and other leaders of the A.U.A. in the twentieth century. Yet it is understandable that it might have appeared to them as a personal affront. Cornish, especially, felt sensitive about it. But Eliot was enthusiastic about the concept of an appraisal, and during his administration, in the early 1920s, one had been conducted.

A special nominating committee selected the members of the Commission. The Reverend Frank O. Holmes, committee member representing the Unitarian Ministerial Union, suggested that the chairman be Frederick May Eliot, minister of Unity Church in St. Paul. He was appointed; and this was a decision with far-reaching consequences for the denomination.

Others selected were the following: the Reverend James Luther Adams, minister of the Unitarian Society of Wellesley Hills; Walter Pritchard Eaton, professor of drama at Yale University; Eduard C. Lindeman, of the faculty of the New York School of Social Work; Frederick G. Melcher, editor of *Publisher's Weekly,* New York; James Bissett Pratt, professor of philosophy, Williams College; and Aurelia Henry Reinhardt, president of Mills College, former president of the American Association of University Women. Samuel P. Capen, chancellor of the University of Buffalo, served on the commission as a consultant. Two staff members were also selected: H. Paul Douglass, author of the *St. Louis Church Survey,*[4] as director of studies; and John J. Hader, technical assistant. Two of the commission members were non-Unitarians: Pratt and Lindeman. None was a denominational official. Only two were ministers: Eliot and Adams. Adams was the only member from Greater Boston.

Their report was wide ranging, with analyses both of Unitarian values and of organizational structure. Certain of the major conclusions dealt perceptively with the relationship between the two. Unitarians, it was noted, have traditionally enjoyed a wide range of value-expressions; therefore "a rigid concept of organization would be totally unthinkable." This characteristic of the movement has tended to cause the constituency to devalue outward forms of organization, thereby allowing conflict between centripetal and centrifugal forces to be unrestrained. In the face of such centrifugal forces as strong individualism, evidenced in the personal religious values of the constituency, and the existence of autonomous lay organizations, the response of the administrative staff of the A.U.A., it was asserted, had been excessive centralization.

Recommendations of the report included such structural innovations as a permanent commission on planning and review, and a moderator. But at the heart of the recommendations was an insistence that the sense of participation of the entire constituency must be increased:

> A group that has so long been accustomed to highly individualistic methods must *learn* to act cooperatively. It has to re-educate itself. It must become organization-conscious, through writing and discussion about the subject, and through conferences designed to show the importance of acting organically.[5]

In the annual meeting of 1936, certain specific votes respecting organization were requested by the Commission of Appraisal, and steps were taken to initiate changes in the by-laws of the Association. The reception of the report, and the overwhelming support for the particular votes requested, made it clear that the Unitarian constituency was ready to move ahead in the direction marked out.

Yet as important as the blueprint for the future was the leadership that would be required. The quadrennial election of a president of the A.U.A. was scheduled for the following year. "In our judgment," declared the Appraisal Commission, "the time is ripe for vigorous leadership that shall create and mobilize the backing among our people which a policy of administrative decentralization would require."[6]

Frederick May Eliot was such a leader.

II

As a result of his work as chairman of the Commission of

Appraisal, Frederick May Eliot became for many a symbol of a renewed vigor for Unitarianism. Leslie Pennington has recalled that he was "for my generation of men the man who epitomized the finest elements in Unitarianism." [7] It was his destiny to lead the denomination in a new period of Unitarian growth, and to usher in the Unitarian renaissance. [8]

Eliot, the inheritor of a distinguished family background, was the son, nephew, and grandson of Unitarian ministers. His father, the Reverend Christopher Rhodes Eliot, was minister of the First Church in Dorchester, and later minister of Bulfinch Place Church, Boston. His uncle, Thomas Lamb Eliot, served as minister in Portland, Oregon, where he was instrumental in founding Reed College. His grandfather, William Greenleaf Eliot, Jr., was for more than half a century minister and minister emeritus of the Church of the Messiah in St. Louis, and for a dozen years served as chancellor of Washington University, of which he was one of the founders. Frederick's mother was Mary Jackson May, and there were Unitarian ministers on her side of the family as well, among them his great-uncle, Samuel May, Jr., of Leicester, Massachusetts, who was the general agent of the Massachusetts Anti-Slavery Society for almost twenty years.

On graduating from Harvard in 1911, Eliot was drawn both to the field of government and to the ministry. He spent the academic year 1911-12 in Europe, studying municipal government; and his strong interest in public affairs and his concern for problems of administration continued throughout his life. But in the course of the year abroad, he definitely decided on the ministry. In the fall of 1912, he entered the Harvard Divinity School, graduating with an S.T.B. degree in 1915. He was ordained on May 16, 1915, and began two years as associate minister with Dr. Samuel McChord Crothers at the First Parish in Cambridge. On June 15, 1915, he was married to Elizabeth Berkeley Lee.

In 1917, he was called to Unity Church, St. Paul, where he remained for more than twenty years. He was happy in St. Paul, and turned aside several opportunities to go elsewhere, including: a position in the department of religious education at headquarters in Boston; a call to Chicago, First Church, in 1922; a combined appointment at the Harvard Divinity School and the Cambridge church, in 1925; and in 1928, a call to be Dr. Crothers's successor in Cambridge. The St. Paul church thrived under his leadership, and at one time, a group of citizens earnestly solicited him to be a candidate for mayor of the city.

Eliot's roots had struck deeply in St. Paul when, in the eyes of many Unitarians, his services as chairman of the Commission of Appraisal made him the obvious choice to succeed Cornish as president of the A.U.A. Eliot himself felt that just because he had headed the commission it would be improper for him to allow his name to be considered. "To do so," he wrote to Leslie Pennington, "would, it seems to me, throw serious doubt, in the minds of many people, on the disinterestedness of the motives which have prompted my activity in denominational affairs during the last two or three years." [9] Pennington responded with a letter that ranks among the most important documents in recent Unitarian history. Convinced that Eliot was the one man in the denomination who could give it the kind of leadership needed, Pennington marshalled the arguments for Eliot's acceptance with extraordinary skill and understanding of what would be required to break down Eliot's resistance.[10] In November, 1936, the board of directors unanimously reaffirmed an earlier decision to nominate Eliot; and after several weeks of indecision, Eliot consented.

Eliot was not to be the only candidate, for a while, at any rate. Forces were at work to bring about the nomination by petition of Dr. Charles R. Joy, Cornish's administrative vice president. A bitter contest began to develop, in which, among other things, Eliot was accused of being a Humanist. For about a month, in April, 1937, committees supporting each candidate marshalled their forces and prepared statements and counter-statements. Early in May, however, Joy withdrew his candidacy, feeling that the true issues had become obscured. Wishing for harmony in the denomination, he said: "If in any way I have misrepresented Dr. Eliot, I am sincerely sorry. I hope that his administration may be happy, fruitful, and blessed of God." [11]

III

The new spirit of enthusiasm in the Unitarian denomination in the spring of 1937 may be attributed to several factors: (1) the end of the controversy raised by Charles Joy's nomination; (2) a feeling of greater freedom for theological dialogue, giving the Humanists a greater sense of belonging to the fellowship;[12] (3) the acceptance of the report of the Interim Commission[13] and the approval of new by-laws for the Association, thereby opening the way to a more dynamic program; and (4) an upsurge of morale among ministers and laymen alike, rallying behind the dynamic strength and promise of rejuvenation symbolized by the new leader.

The Interim Commission, which operated in 1936-37, had essentially five main purposes behind its proposed changes in the by-laws:

1. To strengthen the democratic control over the policies and work of the Association by increasing the powers of the delegate meetings, both the Annual Meeting in Boston and the biennial General Conference meeting elsewhere.
2. To strengthen the Board of Directors as the chief agent for the Association between delegate meetings, in the determining of policies and in the general supervision of the work.
3. To introduce a larger element of lay leadership into the life of the denomination.
4. To make the executive staff more directly responsible to the Board of Directors and more efficient in its actual operation.
5. To enable the Board of Directors to inaugurate a policy to promote regional responsibility.[14]

The approval by the delegates at the Annual Meeting in 1937 of revisions to the bylaws, substantially as proposed by the Appraisal Commission, was a ratification of these purposes.

When the delegates assembled for the General Conference in October at Niagara Falls, they had an opportunity to hear Dr. Eliot address them directly concerning significant trends in the denomination. He spoke of a renewed spiritual emphasis and the importance of theology, mentioning the Greenfield group and a Humanist Seminar as activities evidencing more productive scholarship. In urging a wider fellowship, he emphasized closer cooperation with Universalists, and joint projects in social action to be undertaken with the Society of Friends. He stated:

In the next few years I anticipate an increasing centering of attention upon an educational campaign among us to awaken Unitarians everywhere to the need for developing a rational program of social action that will be in complete harmony with our traditions. It will, in my opinion, be very different from anything we have had in the past; and it will serve as a unifying rather than a divisive force among us.[15]

He indicated that the most obvious change of policy that the denomination had recently made was a shift from centralized administration in the direction of greater regional responsibility, thereby democratizing the Association. He urged an aggressive extension program:

> It is time for Unitarians to adopt the adjective "aggressive" in think-ing and talking about their denominational program—especially in the field of church extension. We can have an aggressive policy with-out intolerance or arrogance or bad manners; and the risk of being misunderstood is less than the risk of being overlooked. . . . The re-sults of this part of our program will determine the whole question of our future.[16]

He reminded the delegates of a basic commitment:

> Deep down underneath, there are two factors without which none of this constructive work can be done—denominational loyalty, and the spirit of sacrificial giving. Without these, no program can be carried out, no ideal achieved. . . . in both these matters Unitarians have in recent years been woefully remiss. . . .
> We are becoming aware of our own greatness. We are feeling the stir and thrill of new confidence. We are becoming a Church. And loyalty and sacrifice will not be demanded of us in vain.[17]

Eliot outlined three immediate goals for the year. The first of them concerned the new hymnal, *Hymns of the Spirit,* which was ready for distribution that month. He proposed a goal of 20,000 copies in use by May. Secondly, he hoped that the 3,300 sub-scriptions to the *Christian Register* would be doubled in the same period. Finally, he urged an increase in annual giving to the Association. In 1937, the amount was $25,836.97, or an average of twenty-five cents per person. For 1938, he proposed $45,000 as a goal, and declared that the projected $19,000 increase would be used for church extension.[18]

Soon the characteristic emphases of the new administration began to emerge, and creative developments were undertaken, notably in two areas: religious education and humanitarian service.

(1) *Religious Education.* Dr. Eliot had long been concerned about religious education. His first published book, *The Unwrought Iron,* was the outgrowth of his discussion classes at the First Parish in Cambridge; while at St. Paul, he had initiated special programs which made extensive use of the creative arts and included a Saturday session. The Report of the Commission of Appraisal went so far as to argue that the entire church program should be redefined in terms of education.

When Eliot took office in 1937, the secretary of the department of religious education was Ernest W. Kuebler, appointed two years earlier. A graduate of Boston University, Kuebler had done graduate work both there and at Yale. Before his appointment, he had been director of religious education at a Congregational church in Newton, Massachusetts. Young and forward looking, with Eliot's backing and with the assistance of a talented group of writers, Kuebler began to reshape the curricular materials published by the Association for Unitarian Sunday schools. At the time of his appointment in 1935, he had indicated the direction that religious education must follow:

A recent writer . . . suggests for our consideration, thus: that the Sunday School must be freed from the conventional routines and programs; that the length of time that the learner is under direct religious influence must be increased; that more of the normal life of the growing child must be brought into the church school; that the isolation of the church school from other educational agencies must be broken. Then, and then only, can results be expected.[19]

The key figure in reconstructing the curriculum proved to be Sophia L. Fahs, who was appointed editor of children's materials in 1937.[20] She brought to the work a rich experience both in the theory and in the practice of religious education, having taught at Union Theological Seminary, and served on the staff of the Riverside Church School, in New York. When she took up her duties with the Association, she was sixty-one years of age. Originally from an orthodox religious background, she had first encountered the Unitarians when, in the course of a survey of the religious education materials of several denominations, she made a study of the Beacon Course, the Unitarian curriculum developed in the first decades of the century. Later, in 1930, she had been an invited speaker at Star Island.

The first of the books in the New Beacon Series was *Beginnings of Earth and Sky* (1937), in which creation stories from many lands were brought together with a scientific account of the immensity of the universe. Other segments of the projected new curriculum included a series of biographies and a fresh treatment of biblical materials. But none of the texts gained wider acceptance, both within and without Unitarian circles, than the *Martin and Judy* books, in which situations with religious overtones within the experience of children were explored. There were three of them, the product of collaboration between Verna Hills and Mrs. Fahs. Among others who produced titles for the New Beacon Series were Dorothy T. Spoerl, Elizabeth Manwell, and Florence Klaber. But Mrs. Fahs was the one indispensable figure, and her contribution has been summarized thus by a recent commentator:

> The new Beacon Series in Religious Education emerged out of, and was a synthesis of, the liberal movement in theology, the progressive movement in education, and the critical movement in Biblical studies. In the figure of Sophia Lyon Fahs, the synthesis found articulation at precisely the moment when the American Unitarians were seeking a curriculum editor. The appointment of Mrs. Fahs in 1937 was the crucial event in the modern history of Unitarian religious education. In its way it was more important than Channing's address on the Sunday School in 1837, for whereas Channing only announced a revolution, Mrs. Fahs effected one.[21]

(2) *The Service Committee.* A committee to aid Czechoslovakian Unitarians, which arrived in Prague before the Nazis did in the fall of 1938, was the embryo from which the Unitarian Service Committee grew. Shortly after the Munich Pact was signed and Chamberlain uttered his famous remark about "peace in our time," Boston Unitarians held a meeting with local Czechoslovakians to discuss what aid could be given to their brothers overseas. Immense concern was expressed over the Czechoslovakian tragedy. Within a very short time, the wheels were set in motion for Czech aid. Dr. Frank O. Holmes has recalled "how quickly Eliot acted, so that Unitarians beat Hitler there." [22]

Seth T. Gano, Boston corporation executive and trustee, was chosen chairman of the committee for Czech relief. Before long, he was on his way with Dr. Robert C. Dexter, head of the A.U.A. Department of Social Relations, and Richard Wood of the Friends

Sophia Lyon Fahs   *Frederick May Eliot*

Service Committee, to investigate the situation on the spot. Although the initial impetus for the organization of the committee was to give aid to Unitarian Czechs, the work soon broadened out, and, in coöperation with the Quakers, became nonsectarian.

The refugee work led in turn to the formation, two years later, of the Unitarian Service Committee, which Dr. Eliot once asserted was "the most important Unitarian event in this century." The original officers of the Service Committee, announced at the annual meeting of the A.U.A. in 1940, were: chairman, Dr. William Emerson, formerly dean of the School of Architecture at M.I.T.; vice-chairman, Seth T. Gano; and executive director, Dr. Robert Dexter. Members of the committee were: Dr. Winfred Overholser, superintendent of St. Elizabeth's Hospital, Washington, D.C., and former president of the American Psychiatric Association; Alfred F. Whitman, of the Children's Aid Society of Boston; Harold H. Burton, mayor of Cleveland; J. Harry Hooper, minister of the Old Ship Church, Hingham, Massachusetts; Louise

L. Wright (Mrs. Quincy Wright), chairman, Department of Government and Foreign Policy, League of Women Voters; Percival Brundage, of the firm of Price, Waterhouse & Co.; and Edward B. Witte, prominent Unitarian layman.

Two commissioners, Waitstill Sharp and his wife, Martha, were scheduled to go to France and work among the 50,000 Czech refugees there; but France capitulated on the day they were scheduled to sail from New York. Instead, four days later they flew to Lisbon and established headquarters there. In September, Dr. Charles R. Joy joined them. One of the dramatic events of these exciting days was the rescue of the German novelist, Lion Feuchtwanger, who was being sought by Nazi agents. Sharp brought him to the United States in October, 1940, using Mrs. Sharp's ticket. Soon after his arrival, Feuchtwanger spoke before the Unitarian Club of Boston, telling of his escape "disguised as an old lady complete with shawl and dark glasses." [23] He described the despair that he, and others like him, had felt:

> Helpless and bound, we feared to be forgotten, stagnant water split from the stream of life; we feared to be left to anonymous annihilation; and this fear paralyzed us and filled our nights with despair. . .
>
> Even today it seems like a dream when I think of the hour, long before sunrise, when secretive and conspiring, I drove to a gloomy station. There I addressed a total stranger, known to me by description only, introduced myself to him under an assumed name which, for the next few weeks, had to be my name, and that stranger—he was your Mr. Sharp—answered "Fine. Splendid that you have come. Now let's go." And so, he took my fate into his hands. [24]

Feuchtwanger's expressions of gratitude and account of details of the escape were so widely publicized that there were unfortunate consequences. A vice-consul at Marseilles, who had helped with the escape, was transferred, and use of this underground method had to be discontinued.

At the end of 1940, Martha Sharp returned to America, having completed her project of bringing twenty-eight children from France to Portugal for passage to the United States. The refugee children—Czech, German, Austrian, and French—sailed on December 13, and were placed in American homes. Dr. Joy had now taken the place of the Sharps. One case of many that he handled involved a child whom he helped to get out of France into Portugal:

The problem involved many wires, a trip by an agent to this boy's home, the expenditure of considerable money . . . and the usual amount of difficulties with visas, which Martha took care of. But we brought the boy out, and when I got off the train, I was embraced (not by the mother) but by the former Austrian Consul to Rio Janeiro, who was much interested in the case, and whose eyes were filled with tears of joy, and so warmly thanked by the excited mother, that I felt it had all been worth while.[25]

IV

Dr. Eliot had just begun his second four-year term as president of the Association when the United States entered the war. Priorities for the first term had been the rebuilding of morale, support for new developments in religious education, and the strengthening of regional organization. But beyond these concerns, anticipated by the Appraisal Commission report, events had called into being the Service Committee and forced Unitarians to broaden the scope of their humanitarian involvement. Eliot's second term was largely dominated by the priorities imposed by the war effort and the search for a basis for a more durable peace.

Eliot insisted that Unitarians carry on in a spirit of optimism, and that the work of the church was more important than ever. But the war presented difficulties for usual operations. Official correspondence of the period is full of references to ministers away as chaplains, parishioners engaged in war work on the home front or away in the service, gas rationing, and restrictions on summer conferences and other assemblies. The May Meetings in 1943 were much abbreviated, and the November General Conference meeting that year was *pro forma* only, to meet requirements of the by-laws. In May, 1945, the meeting of the A.U.A. was likewise *pro forma*.

By April, 1943, twenty-four ministers were serving as chaplains, with more scheduled to leave for duty soon. Local churches were drained of their younger leaders, and older members carried burdens that ordinarily would have been shifted to more vigorous shoulders. In November, 1943, a number of the churches sponsored advertisements in the *Christian Register*, in which they listed members on their service rolls; some of the impact of the war on local church life may be appreciated when one notes, for example, 105 names on the Concord, Massachusetts, list, or 137 from Cleveland, Ohio. From a church in the Southwest, Eliot received this typical comment:

> We do, however, face the problem of a somewhat smaller average attendance, and an older group. We have to face the fact that more than thirty-five of our people, most of them young, are in the army or in war service. Added to this is the tire and gas situation, victory gardens, and the fact that a large number of our women are now employed and Sunday is the only day they have for their home duties.[26]

Churches found themselves engaged in new forms of community service. Thus in Oklahoma City a Teen Time meeting was organized which attracted young people from all walks of life and diverse religious traditions, and served the needs of young service men in particular.

The war brought added strains at headquarters, just about doubling the duties of the staff, at the same time that a reduction in force was necessary. "One of our men," Eliot noted, "returned not long ago from a six-weeks trip up and down the Pacific Coast and reported a fifteen pound loss in weight!" [27]

In 1942, the board of directors of the A.U.A. sent a message of greeting to all the churches, in which it was urged that "the immediate duty of every church should be to make the utmost possible contribution to the defeat of the Axis powers." [28] At the same time, the denomination at large and the board of directors in particular were much more sensitive to the claims of conscientious objection than had been the case in the first World War. Memories were still fresh of the annual meeting in 1936, when the Association had expressed regret for the action of the board in 1918 in using economic pressures against pacifist ministers in the denomination. Dr. Eliot himself was not a pacifist; but he was deeply concerned that the rights of pacifists be protected.

At a meeting of the board on January 12, 1944, it was reported that there had been considerable expense involved in supporting pacifists in civilian public service camps, and that the burden had fallen largely on the historic peace churches. Eliot reminded the board of the number of times when this matter had come before it, and of the small amount of help the Association had given. He reported recent action by several denominations, notably the

Presbyterians and Episcopalians, in establishing commissions to raise money to meet their share of the expense. The board responded by assigning to its War Service Council—already set up for service to chaplains and other members of the armed forces— the duty of maintaining a list of Unitarian conscientious objectors, and providing assistance to them. Later that year, the board passed a resolution to place on record the Unitarian position on conscientious objection, of which the key clauses were the following:

> *Now therefore be it resolved,* that any Unitarian who has so registered with said American Unitarian Association shall be entitled to a certificate to that effect in claiming exemption as a conscientious objector, and
> *Be it further resolved,* that any avowed Unitarian claiming to be a conscientious objector is within the purview of Unitarian principles; and
> *Be it further resolved,* that any avowed Unitarian shall be entitled upon request to a copy of this resolution for use before any Selective Service Board, and any Court before which the question of his status as a conscientious objector is pending.[29]

During the war, the work of the Service Committee was expanded in variety and scope. From the time of the fall of France in 1940 until the allied liberation in 1944, the Committee's chief overseas headquarters was in Lisbon, where at various times Mr. and Mrs. Sharp, Dr. Joy, Mr. and Mrs. Robert C. Dexter, and the Reverend and Mrs. Howard L. Brooks directed relief work among refugees. They were instrumental in assisting to freedom scores of exiles from Nazi persecution, among them many intellectuals, including a Nobel prize winner. For a time, under the direction of Noel Field, refugees were assisted at Marseilles; but when the Nazis took over unoccupied France, Field was forced to move his base of operations to Geneva. In 1944, following the Allied invasion, he was smuggled back into France by the Maquis, the French partisan organization. It is believed that he was the first official of a private relief agency to return to France. By January, 1945, an office had been opened in Paris by Mme. Herta Tempi. Work was also undertaken in Toulouse among Spanish refugees —Loyalists from the Spanish Civil War. And in 1945, a medical mission was sent to Italy to study problems of malnutrition and starvation, and to lay the foundation for work to be carried on by

Italian medical personnel. (In the post-war years, medical missions were a significant and distinctive technique by which a relatively small denomination used limited resources to maximum effect.) In the United States, the Service Committee sponsored home service projects, including summer work camps in which Unitarian young people participated, especially under the leadership of the newly reorganized American Unitarian Youth, of which G. Richard Kuch was the president.

Unitarians were, of course, not solely concerned with the immediate problems of the war, but were at the same time planning ahead for the years that would follow. The threat of Nazism encouraged in the free world a good deal of soul-searching and rethinking of the meaning of democracy and the means of preserving it. These themes recurred so often during the May Meetings of 1942 that the *Register* published a special section of addresses delivered to various groups and sessions, the titles of which tell the story of a sharply focused concern: "Blueprints for Democracy," "Democracy as a Modern Religion," "The Religious Basis for the New World Order," "Presuppositions of Democracy." [30] Nazi racial theories and racial unrest in the United States in 1943 were a reminder of unfinished business on the agenda of the democracies. "A world in which one race thinks of itself as 'superior' cannot be a world of coöperative peace and order," wrote Dr. Eliot; " a world in which one religion thinks of itself as 'the religion' cannot overcome race prejudice." [31] Seldom in Unitarian history has the attempt been more consciously made to articulate the relationship between religious liberalism and political democracy.

The usual work of church extension was much curtailed during the war, though a few new churches were gathered, notably one named for Thomas Jefferson in Charlottesville, Virginia. In 1944, the A.U.A. Board voted to establish the Unitarian Church of the Larger Fellowship in order to serve isolated religious liberals who had no opportunity to join a local church. Dr. Albert C. Dieffenbach was named minister, and he laid plans to set up membership rolls and maintain contact with members by means of a monthly pastoral letter and the distribution of denominational publications. "Besides these things," he announced, "the minister will perform most of the services that belong to a pastor in a local parish. The religious education of the children in the home is provided by the church in excellent courses of instruction." [32] When Dieffenbach reported to the board just over two years later, he was able to record a steadily increasing membership, which then stood at 775, with a constituency of 1500. Every state in the Union was represented, and several Canadian provinces. In the Canal Zone, eight individual members had come together to form the "Balboa Chapter" of the Church of the Larger Fellowship.

Meanwhile, planning for denominational expansion after the war went on under the rubric of "Unitarian Advance." An early product of this planning was a widely circulated "declaration of faith and purpose," entitled "The Faith Behind Freedom," presented at May Meetings in 1943. This document, couched in elevated language, defined human experience to have been the struggle to be free "from the limitations in the natural world . . . , from fear and ignorance, and from the tyrannies imposed by other men." It proclaimed that "freedom grows from free religion, that only a free religion can be universal, and that every other freedom is based on freedom of the mind." It avowed a faith that humanity "has the power of moral growth," and repudiated "the fear . . . that human progress has resulted in insoluble dilemmas." It expressed a purpose "to build a World Community of free and equal men, dedicated to equality of human rights and obligations, and governed by the laws that free men make." And it acknowledged that to proclaim noble purposes is not the same thing as achieving them. "Mankind is buying, with its blood and agony, the chance to build a better world. Let us begin to build it. The time of opportunity is now." [33]

Three committees were set up to plan for Unitarian advance after the war. They were based on recommendations to the board made in May, 1943, by the advisory council of the division of promotion and publications, which in turn relied on a report by Hamilton Warren of New York, a member of the board, entitled: "How to Extend Liberal Religion." Committee A, with A. Powell Davies as chairman, was intended as a "creative" committee, primarily to explore ideas that unite Unitarians, and to work with a great deal of freedom in what might be called "brainstorming." Committee B, of which Warren became chairman, was a practical committee, or "testing-and-methods" committee, to suggest ways to extend liberal religion. Committee C was appointed somewhat later, with Raymond Bragg as chairman. It consisted of organizational representatives of groups within or affiliated with the Association, and was "to study the possibility of closer integration of the organizations of the Unitarian fellowship." [34]

Committee A directed its attention to the preparation of a statement defining the Unitarian position, which the board accepted, though not without dissent, as providing a basis for Unitarian Advance. But of more practical consequence, as it turned out, was a recommendation from Committee B to restructure the Association's publications program. At the meeting of the board on January 10, 1945, it was voted to employ "a thoroughly competent executive to have charge of the public relations program of the Association and to invite the other principal Unitarian bodies to participate in a united public relations program for the entire denomination under his general direction." [35] What made this significant was that on July 1, 1945, Melvin Arnold became director of the newly-established division of public relations.

V

From war, America moved into the period of cold war, as many Americans became suspicious of the intentions of their recent Soviet allies. In foreign affairs, the Truman administration adopted a policy of containment of Soviet power, together with aid to the nations of the free world to help them rebuild their strength. Once again, as before the war, American leftist groups came under suspicion if their position seemed to be an obedient echo of Stalinist policy. In this proto-McCarthy era, liberals concerned to promote international friendship and to diminish Soviet-American tensions ran the risk of being called fellow-travelers, if not actually Communists. The Unitarians found themselves in this situation in 1946 and 1947, partly because the Service Committee had done refugee work among leftist intellectuals, and partly because of controversy over the *Christian Register*. This controversy was potentially very disruptive within the denomination, and was a major crisis of the Eliot Administration.

The *Christian Register*, for more than a century a wholly independent weekly, in the 1930s became dependent on subsidies from the A.U.A. In 1939, because of the growing deficit, the Association assumed ownership, and made the journal a semimonthly, continuing the services of Llewellyn Jones as editor. Eighteen months later, another drastic change took place: editorial control was placed in the hands of officers of the Association; Jones's services were terminated; and the magazine became a monthly. Eliot was sharply criticized at the annual meeting in 1941 as a result, the accusation being that, in the nature of things, the *Register* could be little more than a house organ, reflecting the policies of the Administration. Eliot acknowledged that the *Register* would be the "official organ" of the A.U.A., and that the officers of the Association would be responsible for what appeared in its columns. But he expressed confidence that it could reflect "the thought and aspirations of our fellowship of free churches" as effectively under the guidance of the officers and staff of the Association as by a theoretically "independent" editor. He particularly covenanted that the columns would remain open to critical articles and letters.[36]

In 1943, Stephen H. Fritchman was appointed editor. He was already a member of the headquarters staff, serving as adviser to American Unitarian Youth. Under his direction, the *Register* was a lively magazine, and the circulation increased steadily. While the paper had never been limited to purely denominational concerns, the attention given to public issues perceptibly increased under Fritchman's editorship. Some Unitarians felt that a house organ, owned and edited by the Association, was not the best forum for the discussion of political issues. But Fritchman had the full backing of the Eliot administration.

In May, 1946, Fritchman was accused of being a Communist and of using the pages of the *Register* as a vehicle to espouse the communist cause. A long and bitter controversy ensued. Eliot defended his staff member and friend against incredible pressure until, in the spring of 1947, Fritchman refused to be censored by administrative control of the *Register*—or, as Eliot and others interpreted it, to continue to coöperate with the editorial advisory board, which had been established to work with him on editorial content. On May 20, 1947, the board of directors of the A.U.A. voted to terminate his employment as editor. He had earlier resigned as A.U.Y. director to devote full time to the editorial department of the division of publications.

Fritchman took his case to the May Meetings. The debate in Boston was long and tense over a motion to recommend to the board of directors that they reinstate Fritchman as editor of the *Register* on a basis to be worked out. The motion lost. Eliot, barely able to speak, his voice choked with emotion, did, however, address the delegates at length. He said:

> I would like to be defending Stephen Fritchman as I have consistently, for more than twelve months, and it's Mr. Fritchman's refusal to coöperate with us in a friendly spirit that has made it necessary for us to say he has broken down the arrangement and we have got to find some other way.

Eliot never lost his affection for Fritchman, and Fritchman never lost his affection for Eliot.[37]

In 1948, Fritchman became minister of the First Unitarian Church of Los Angeles, where he served for more than two decades. In 1969, Dr. Fritchman received the Holmes-Weatherly Award for his "driving passion for economic, social and political justice."

While the attention of Unitarians in 1946 and 1947 was focused to a large extent on the Fritchman controversy, other developments of great consequence to the future of the denomination were moving forward. Specifically, the late 1940s and early 1950s saw the rebirth of the Beacon Press and the development of Unitarian fellowships.

(1) *The Beacon Press.* When Melvin Arnold became director of the division of publications in 1945, he was responsible, among other things, for the Beacon Press. In ten years' time, he transformed it from a minor adjunct of the A.U.A.'s work into a widely recognized voice for liberal religion.[38]

Edward Darling, assistant director of the division of publications at that time, has described the situation shortly after Arnold's arrival thus:

The first new catalog was published in the spring of 1948. The "backlist" at that time was composed of 19 books. Nineteen. Nineteen books on the active list! Of these, two were hymnbooks (*Beacon Song & Service;* and *Hymns of the Spirit*). Seventeen "trade" books, then. Of these, six were what you'd call full-length books. All the rest of them were collections of sermons without any central theme, usually quite thin volumes. For the general book trade in America, where books are sold over the counters, there were not more than four: Davies, *American Destiny;* Patton, *Hello, Man;* Pierce, *The Soul of the Bible;* and Wilbur, *Our Unitarian Heritage.*[39]

Arnold's immediate efforts went into attracting to Beacon Press authors whose books might be expected to appeal to the general trade. In the first two years, Pitirim A. Sorokin, Albert Schweitzer, John Dewey, and Bronislaw Malinowski were among those added to the Beacon list. All this was done on a shoestring, with no capital behind the venture. As Darling put it: "Beacon had no sales organization, no direct mail operation, no money for advertising, no backlist to support new publishing. In the light of the experience, . . . one would say that historically, fiscally, and in any practical terms, Beacon Press was an impossibility." [40]

The breakthrough came with the publication of Paul Blanshard's *American Freedom and Catholic Power* on April 19, 1949 —one of the most controversial and successful books Beacon has ever handled. It detailed Catholic positions—pre-Vatican II positions, one should remember—on matters such as public versus parochial schools, birth control, divorce, and the censorship of literature and the movies, analyzing the threat posed to traditional American democrcay. It was a book most publishers would not touch, particularly textbook publishers, who were fearful lest other books on their lists be subject to boycott.

The decision to publish Blanshard's book was not made without some hesitation and concern as to possible consequences. Some of those involved worried lest it encourage old fashioned anti-Catholic bigotry; others wondered if it might invite some kind of retaliation. But Arnold sought to protect the Press by checking and double-checking the manuscript for factual errors. Copies in mimeographed form were circulated to scholars throughout the world, and many corrections were made; galley proofs and page proofs were checked by specialists. Unbound books were sent in advance of publication to Catholic headquarters and other possible critics. Finally, the jacket of the book gave notice that if mistakes were found, Beacon Press would make corrections for the next printing, upon receiving documentation of the error.

Arnold had no way of guessing how successful the book might be, and authorized a first printing of 4,000 copies. They were sold out within a day or two. Sales were running at about 1,000 copies a week in May and June; but when Cardinal Spellman and Mrs. Roosevelt clashed over the issue of federal aid to church-connected schools, the figure jumped to 2,000. One week, more than 6,000 copies were sold. There were twenty-six printings of the first edition; and in all, the book sold about a third of a million copies.[41]

It was now possible for Beacon to expand its publishing program. It became known for other ventures, including several volumes on Church-State issues; several dealing with Albert Schweitzer; and, in 1952, Jack Anderson and Ronald May's *McCarthy: The Man, The Senator, The "Ism."* It was one of the first publishers to enter the field of "quality" paperbacks. In 1956, when Arnold resigned to become associate editor of the religious books department of Harper and Brothers, instead of a backlist of 19 titles, Beacon Press had one of 321. It was no longer an obscure adjunct to a small denominational headquarters, but held a secure place in American publishing with a reputation for both courage and integrity.

(2) *Unitarian Fellowships.* If the Beacon Press was one of the major successes of the postwar years the other was the development of lay-led religious groups, or "fellowships." This development began with a vote by the Board of Directors of the A.U.A. on March 14, 1945, to consider the idea of "organizing lay centers in communities where there is no Unitarian church and where there is a sufficient number of individual Unitarians." [42] The first such group was admitted to affiliation with the A.U.A. in 1948. Ten years later, there were 249 of them, and twenty years later, almost 500.

Lay-led religious groups are not a Unitarian invention; and even in Unitarian circles, there were precedents for the fellowship movement. As far back as 1895, Jabez T. Sunderland had argued for the "establishment of religious Sunday Circles, or what I may call simple parlor churches, in a hundred—yes in five hundred—communities where there are now no liberal religious churches or services." In Dr. Samuel A. Eliot's early years as president of the Association, an attempt had been made to organize the "Unitarian League of Lay Centers." The device had not caught on, however, apparently because the plan on which the centers were to be established was lacking in flexibility, and not conducive to the development of local initiative. More recently, the Reverend Lon Ray Call, who was minister-at-large in the department of Unitarian extension, had had direct contact with the problems that arise in local situations, and was convinced from personal experience that, with careful preparation, such groups could be successful. At any rate, they would involve less financial risk to the Association than the old method of church extension, which relied on full-time clerical leadership, subsidized at headquarters for an extended period of time.[43]

The study committee appointed in 1945 was stirred to action by a report prepared by Call in 1946. At headquarters the awareness soon grew that groups of the type under consideration were beginning to spring up spontaneously. In 1947, the board authorized a permanent working committee on "lay units," and funds were assigned for the appointment of a director. Early in 1948, Munroe C. Husbands, himself a layman, was named to the post.

Husbands's task was not to bring such scattered groups under control, but to facilitate their birth, allowing them to find their own identity, develop their own style, and produce their own leadership. His procedure was to locate a nucleus of unattached religious liberals in a given community, to bring them together, and to assist in the early phases of organization. Having drawn up a statement of purpose and adopted by-laws, and made a financial contribution to the A.U.A., the group would apply for status as a fellowship. In terms of congregational polity as historically understood, such a group is a "church"; in terms of the administrative categories useful to the Unitarian bureaucracy, the "fellowship" is distinguished from the "church" in that normatively it is small and relies on lay rather than professional leadership.

Some, perhaps most, of those who watched the early develop-ment of the fellowship movement assumed that fellowships were supposed to be the embryonic beginnings of full-fledged churches. In actual fact, many fellowships did develop in that direction. In 1967, when Lon Ray Call looked back over the previous twenty years, he noted that eighty "fellowships" had become "churches." But that was not the whole story. Some fellowships had had a short life and disappeared; that was to be expected. What was not generally anticipated was that other groups would decidedly prefer to remain fellowships, that the fellowship experience would be valued more highly than church life. In fellowships that did become churches, the transition was often a difficult one, with strident voices protesting against the successive steps of acquiring property, assuming larger financial obligations, and calling a minister and learning how to live with one.

Clearly, as Laile Bartlett has argued, there was such a thing as the fellowship experience:

> Generally smaller, they have many of the accompanying traits of small-group size: greater intimacy, spontaneity, informality, direct-ness. Do-it-yourself and lay-led, they have a generally higher degree of personal involvement and participation, more identification with group *qua* group, and a greater sense of responsibility for its opera-tion. Fellowship members "join an experience" rather than an in-stitution.[44]

Of course, intimacy and informality have their drawbacks; they do not exhaust the range of human experiences to which religion must be sensitive; they are not for everyone. Dr. Bartlett has recorded the reaction of one Midwest liberal to the fellowship experience: "I've tried one, but to me, they're just a squirmy little pot." Yet the influence of the "fellowship experience" throughout the denomination has been pervasive, even on large and long-established churches, relatively structured and formal in their mode of worship and style of operation. In a period when there has been a widespread revolt against formalism, not exempting ecclesiastical formalism, the fellowships have provided Unitarian-ism with its own home-grown and home-nurtured version of that revolt.[45]

Partly as the result of the fellowship program and partly as a result of more conventional methods of church extension, the numerical growth of the denomination after the war was substantial. Some statistics presented to the Annual Meeting in 1957 illustrate this growth. Adult membership in Unitarian societies increased 53 per cent, from 69,104 in 1947 to an estimated 106,000 in 1957. Church school enrollment gained 169 per cent, from 17,099 in 1947 to an estimated 46,000 in 1957. The number of cities and towns in which there were Unitarian societies increased from 325 to 550. There were no fellowships in 1947; as of May Meetings in 1957 there were 216.[46] Eliot himself was sensitive to the danger of measuring success by quantitative growth alone, but was confident that the growth was sound: "Here are figures that reveal an extraordinary growth," he wrote, "but behind the figures there is a vitality, a freshness of attitude, a confidence of mood and spirit that show promise of future growth beyond anything we have dared to prophesy." [47] This was a time when Protestant churches generally were gaining members; but the percentage gain made by Unitarian churches was one of the highest of all Protestant denominations. Yet at the same time, as Richard Gibbs noted, growth has its costs:

> We are moving out of the cozy family where the leadership could know at least three-quarters of the ministerial leadership on the continent. Obviously we are going to lose the intimacy of the small denomination.[48]

Because it was clear that twenty years of the Eliot Administration had already gone far towards transforming the denomination, the unexpected death of Frederick Eliot seemed in a very striking way to signalize the end of an era. Eliot died in New York on February 17, 1958, while on business related to the Beacon Press, just as he was entering the gate of the Memorial Garden of All Souls Church. No one has stated better than Wallace Robbins the debt the denomination owes to him:

> The presidency of the American Unitarian Association was his great public labor, and few remember at what a lowly point it began. Eight years of national depression had been a coarse abrasive on the churches: financially and spiritually they were scratched and worn. Liberalism was beginning to undergo the counterattack of the re-inspired orthodoxy, and it was theologically an open city.
> In 1937 Frederick, after leading the Commission of Appraisal, came into office, and the weathervanes on every steeple began to turn to a

fresh breeze. From a frightened movement we were transformed into a courageous one. He gave us heart, an intelligent direction, a driving force. Gradually, then with dramatic acceleration, we began to grow under his leadership until today we have caught up with and passed the points of advance of others.

There is at present an explosion in the Unitarian population of our country. This dynamic condition is his living monument, and so history will remember him with growing gratitude.[49]

VI

When Frederick Eliot died at the age of sixty-eight, he was in his twenty-first year as president of the A.U.A., and his current term of office had three years to run. Of the problems he left behind, the most critical were perhaps the closely related ones of merger with the Universalists and a restructuring of the Association to meet the needs of a larger constituency. Some concern had already been expressed, especially in the board of directors, that the burdens of the presidency had become too much for one man and would surely need to be reconsidered when Eliot retired.

It was in the context of this uncertainty about future relationships with the Universalists, and possible redefinition of the office of the presidency, that the successor to Eliot was chosen in May, 1958. The board of directors nominated Ernest W. Kuebler to the position, believing that familiarity with the work at 25 Beacon Street, coupled with his proven administrative ability, would enable him to carry on without loss of momentum through what might be a difficult period of transition. Nominated by petition was the Reverend Dana McLean Greeley, minister of the Arlington Street Church, Boston. Greeley was elected by a vote of 823 to 720, and served as the last president of the A.U.A., until merger was completed three years later. He was then elected to be the first president of the Unitarian Universalist Association.

Discussions leading toward merger were well under way at the time of Frederick Eliot's death. For more than a century, Unitarians and Universalists had related to each other with joint efforts and fraternal warmth. During the 1950s, a partial consolidation of activities pointed toward ultimate organic union. The first groups to reach that goal were the two young people's groups, American Unitarian Youth and the Universalist Youth Fellowship. They voted for merger at joint conventions in June, 1953; and the following year, A.U.Y. and U.Y.F. were dissolved as corporations, to be replaced by Liberal Religious Youth.[50]

Later in the summer of 1953, the Universalist Church of America and the American Unitarian Association met in a joint biennial conference at Andover, Massachusetts. From this meeting a "federal union" emerged in the form of the Council of Liberal Churches (Universalist-Unitarian), created to combine the functions of religious education, publications, and public relations. An interim commission was created at Andover, of which the Reverend Irving R. Murray was chairman, which reported at the next biennial conference in 1955, at Detroit, recommending that total merger be the ultimate aim. The recommendation was endorsed by the delegates of both denominations.

A joint merger commission was then appointed, of which the Reverend William B. Rice was chosen chairman. Its initial task was not to advocate merger, but to study the feasibility of it, and to lay out the alternatives. In September, 1958, it published an "information manual," in which historical, statistical, and organizational data were compiled, to provide a factual basis for discussion. It was accompanied by a "discussion guide" for the use of churches and fellowships in deciding among alternatives. On the basis of very considerable discussion at the local level, a plebiscite in the winter and spring of 1959 indicated that sentiment in both denominations strongly supported organic merger.[51]

With its mandate clarified, the joint merger commission prepared a specific plan for the consolidation of the American Unitarian Association and the Universalist Church of America. The plan was presented to a joint biennial conference of the two denominations, meeting in Syracuse, New York, October 29-31, 1959. The first day, delegates from both denominations met, part of the time in plenary sessions, part of the time in discussion groups, to consider in detail the proposed constitution and by-laws. The climax of the day was a joint session of delegates of both denominations in the evening, which did not adjourn until after one o'clock in the morning. While a number of details of the commission's proposal occasioned debate—regionalism,

Dana McLean Greeley

Munroe Husbands

Stephen Hole Fritchman

A. Powell Davies

annual vs. biennial meetings—the most difficult task of the conference was to resolve once more the perennial problem of Unitarian self-identity—in other words, to restate the purposes of the new organization in such a way as to do justice on the one hand to the sense of continuity with the Christian roots of Unitarianism, and on the other to acknowledge the universal nature of religious truth. That this debate should have taken place in the same city where the "Battle of Syracuse" had been fought in 1866 was a coincidence the significance of which was not lost on the historically-minded. But in a real sense, the "Second Battle of Syracuse" was Syracuse (1866) and Saratoga (1894) combined and condensed into three dramatic and exciting days.[52]

The merger commission itself wavered with respect to the wording of the purposes of the new body. Its original proposal included the clause: "To cherish and spread the universal truths taught by the great prophets and teachers of humanity in every age and tradition, immemorially summarized in their essence as love to God and love to man." The version presented to the delegates in the commission's "first Syracuse report" at the start of the conference introduced a reference to Jesus and the Judeo-Christian tradition. At the beginning of the evening session on the first day, the commission presented its "second Syracuse report," which reverted to the original wording. The arguments made familiar by earlier debates recurred: that "religion is a bigger word than Christian"; and that "universal religion," however appealing it may seem theoretically, does not express the actual religious sensibilities of human beings, and provides no cohesion for religious groups. At the end of the discussion the first day, the vote was to accept the original wording, without Christian or Judeo-Christian references.

The recommendations of the merger commission, as informed by the deliberations of the joint session on Thursday, were reported to separate official meetings of the two denominations on Friday. These sessions were held simultaneously, and the final plan had to be acceptable in every detail to both. The wording of the original proposal was approved by both sessions, though by a sharply divided vote on the Unitarian side. It was evident that the delegates were not yet agreed that the right balance had been found. But it was the Universalists who reconsidered the wording first, voting to insert the words "our Judeo-Christian heritage." On the Unitarian side, the proposal was amended to read "the Judeo-Christian heritage," so that the final wording was as follows: "To cherish and spread the universal truths taught by the great prophets and teachers of humanity in every age and tradition, immemorially summarized in the Judeo-Christian heritage as love to God and love to man." And so by the finest of discriminations, the difference between "our" and "the"—a discrimination of which the Council of Nicea might have been proud —a balance was struck which was the equivalent in 1959 of the consensus an earlier generation had achieved at Saratoga in 1894.

The Syracuse conference in 1959 was decisive for Unitarian-Universalist merger. The plan formulated there was endorsed by Unitarian churches, 555 to 54, and by Universalist churches, 183 to 49. At simultaneous meetings in Boston on May 23, 1960, the proposal was ratified by delegates to the A.U.A. by a vote of 725 to 143; and by delegates to a special General Assembly of the Universalist Church of America, the vote being 365 to 65. The legal steps to consolidate were completed in May, 1961, when the Unitarian Universalist Association was constituted.

The keynote for a new beginning was sounded by the Reverend Donald S. Harrington, at a service of worship in Symphony Hall, Boston, on May 23, 1960, after the final vote had been taken:

> In the milestone moment [he declared], we are led by the significance of the event to take more than customary thought, to reach more urgently for perspective . . .
>
> We stand tonight at such a milestone, one which is partly a birth, partly a commencement, partly a kind of marriage, and which involves also a degree of death, an end of things which have been precious to us and of institutions with which we have been lovingly familiar.
>
> We have achieved a union which is the result of more than a hundred years of striving, and which now, at last, when the time is fully ripe, has come to completion. It is our tremendous potential, born of the world's response to our new relevance, caused by this new world's need for a religion which is dynamic instead of static, unitive instead of divisive, universalistic instead of particularistic, history-making rather than history-bound, that has made this Unitarian-Universalist merger necessary and inevitable.

Then, speaking of the tasks required of religion in the modern world, and the vision of a day yet to be, he concluded:

> May we, Unitarians and Universalists and men and women of good will everywhere, strive with all our might to make our lives, our churches and fellowships, and our new Unitarian Universalist Association the vehicle of this vision![53]

Chapter Notes

NOTES TO THE INTRODUCTION

1. For detailed treatment of this theme, see Conrad Wright, *The Beginnings of Unitarianism in America* (Boston: Starr King Press, c. 1955).
2. The term is that of Ralph Barton Perry, in *Puritanism and Democracy* (New York: Vanguard Press, c. 1944), Chap. 10.
3. Charles Chauncy, *Seasonable Thoughts on the State of Religion in New England* (Boston, 1743), p. 422.
4. See "Rational Religion in Eighteenth-Century America," in Conrad Wright, *The Liberal Christians* (Boston: Beacon Press, c. 1970), pp. 1-21.

CHAPTER ONE NOTES

1. Earl Morse Wilbur, *A History of Unitarianism* (Cambridge, 1952), 2: 394.
2. William B. Sprague, *Annals of the American Unitarian Pulpit* (New York, 1865), p. 164.
3. *The Religious History of New England* (Cambridge, 1917), p. 55.
4. The fullest account of this episode, superseding all previous ones, is Conrad Wright, "The Election of Henry Ware: Two Contemporary Accounts," *Harvard Library Bulletin*, 17 (1969): 245-278.
5. Quoted in Charles H. Lyttle, *The Pentecost of American Unitarianism* (Boston, 1920), p. 8.
6. Quoted in David B. Parke, *The Epic of Unitarianism* (Boston: Starr King Press, 1957), p. 80.
7. *Religious History of New England*, p. 63.
8. William B. Sprague, *The Life of Jedidiah Morse, D.D.* (New York, c. 1874), p. 57.
9. The Unitarian concern for biblical criticism is treated in Jerry W. Brown, *The Rise of Biblical Criticism in America, 1800-1870* (Middletown, Conn.: Wesleyan University Press, c. 1969).

10. Sprague, *Annals*, pp. 405-406.
11. Brown, *Rise of Biblical Criticism*, pp. 10-26.
12. Joseph S. Buckminster, *Sermons* (Boston, 1829), p. 148.
13. Brown, *Rise of Biblical Criticism*, pp. 19ff.
14. Thomas Belsham, *American Unitarianism* (Boston, 1815), p. 4.
15. Jeremiah Evarts, "Review of American Unitarianism," *The Panoplist*, 11 (1815): 250.
16. Sprague, *Jedidiah Morse*, pp. 125-126.
17. William E. Channing, *A Letter to the Rev. Samuel C. Thacher* (Boston, 1815), pp. 13-14.
18. *Ibid.*, pp. 20, 23.
19. The early years of the Divinity School are described in George H. Williams, ed., *The Harvard Divinity School* (Boston: Beacon Press, c. 1954), pp. 21-77.
20. Lyttle, *Pentecost*, pp. 7-9. See also Conrad Wright, ed., *Three Prophets of Religious Liberalism* (Boston: Beacon Press, c. 1961), pp. 5-19.
21. Wright, *Three Prophets*, pp. 49, 55, 52.
22. *Ibid.*, p. 57.
23. *Ibid.*, p. 65.
24. *Ibid.*, pp. 76, 74.
25. Moses Stuart, *Letters to the Rev. Wm. E. Channing* (Andover, 1819); Andrews Norton, *A Statement of Reasons for Not Believing the Doctrines of Trinitarians* (Boston, 1819).
26. The exchange of views was not completed until each author had written three pamphlets.
27. 16 Mass. 488.
28. Joseph S. Clark, *A Historical Sketch of the Congregational Churches in Massachusetts* (Boston, 1858), p. 271.
29. *The Autobiography of Lyman Beecher*, Barbara M. Cross, ed. (Cambridge: Harvard University Press, 1961), 2: 81.
30. Walter Donald Kring, *Liberals among the Orthodox* (Boston: Beacon Press, c. 1974), pp. 29-44.
31. George W. Cooke, *Unitarianism in America* (Boston, 1902), p. 106.
32. For a full account of the founding of the American Unitarian Association, prepared from the original records, see Cooke, *op. cit.*, pp. 127-142. See also Parke, *Epic of Unitarianism*, pp. 100-104.
33. Cooke, *Unitarianism*, p. 139.
34. *Ibid.*, p. 125.

CHAPTER TWO NOTES

1. Henry Ware, Jr., "Sober Thoughts on the State of the Times, Addressed to the Unitarian Community" (1835), *Works* (Boston, 1847), 2: 99.
2. Henry Ware, Jr., "Education the Business of Life" (1837), *Works*, 3: 271-296. Cf. William Ellery Channing, "Remarks on Education" (1833), *Works* (Boston, 1849), 1: 369-387.
3. Cf. Conrad Wright, "From Standing Order to Secularism" (1968), *The Liberal Christians: Essays on American Unitarian History* (Boston: Beacon Press, 1970), p. 116.

4. Horace Mann, "The Necessity of Education in a Republican Government" (1838), *Life and Works,* ed. Mary Mann (Cambridge, Mass., 1867), 2: 143.
5. See Jonathan Messerli, *Horace Mann* (New York: Alfred A. Knopf, 1971).
6. See Paul Goodman, "Ethics and Enterprise: The Values of the Boston Elite," *American Quarterly,* 18 (1966): 437-451, for a fuller discussion.
7. Samuel Eliot Morison, *Three Centuries of Harvard* (Cambridge, Mass.: Harvard University Press, 1936), p. 257.
8. Sydney Ahlstrom, "The Middle Period (1840-80)," *Harvard Divinity School,* ed. George Huntston Williams (Boston: Beacon Press, 1954), pp. 78-147, is very informative.
9. By act of the General Court of Massachusetts, dated April 28, 1865.
10. See Daniel Walker Howe, *The Unitarian Conscience: Harvard Moral Philosophy, 1805-1861* (Cambridge, Mass.: Harvard University Press, 1970).
11. See Lewis P. Simpson, ed., *The Federalist Literary Mind* (Baton Rouge: Louisiana State University Press, 1962), for selections from the *Monthly Anthology.*
12. William Ellery Channing, "Remarks on National Literature" (1830), *Works,* 1: 243-280.
13. Several great nineteenth-century Unitarian historians are treated in David Levin, *History as Romantic Art* (Stanford: Stanford University Press, 1959).
14. Oliver Wendell Holmes, "The Deacon's Masterpiece" (1858), *Works* (Boston, 1892), 12: 417-421.
15. Martin Duberman has written an excellent biography of *James Russell Lowell* (Boston: Houghton Mifflin Co., 1966). A provocative, highly critical essay on the Unitarian contribution to literature is Martin Green, *The Problem of Boston* (New York: W. W. Norton, 1966).
16. Daniel T. McColgan wrote a detailed biography, *Joseph Tuckerman: Pioneer in American Social Work* (Washington, D.C.: Catholic University of America Press, 1940).
17. Joseph Tuckerman, *On the Elevation of the Poor,* ed. Edward Everett Hale (Boston, 1874), is a selection from his reports as minister-at-large.
18. Joseph Tuckerman, *Principles and Results of the Ministry-at-Large* (Boston, 1838), p. 232.
19. Charles Sumner, "The Barbarism of Slavery: Speech in the Senate, June 4, 1860," *Works* (Boston, 1872), 5: 1-174; Charles Sumner, *Argument Against the Constitutionality of Separate Colored Schools in the Case of Roberts v. Boston* (Boston, 1849).
20. Various modes through which Unitarian ministers responded are described in Conrad Wright, "The Minister as Reformer" (1960), *The Liberal Christians,* pp. 62-80. See also Douglas C. Stange, "Patterns of Antislavery among American Unitarians, 1831-1860," Ph.D. dissertation (unpublished), Harvard, 1974.
21. Orville Dewey, "The Slavery Question" (1847; perhaps first delivered earlier), *Works* (Boston, 1893), p. 326; Ezra Stiles Gannett, Thanksgiving Sermon (1830), quoted in William C. Gannett, *Ezra Stiles Gannett: A Memoir* (Boston, 1875), p. 139.
22. Dewey's utterance is quoted and discussed in Wright, *Liberal Christians,* p. 77; Gannett's is quoted in Gannett, *Ezra Stiles Gannett,* p. 301.
23. William Ellery Channing, *Slavery* (1835), in his *Works,* 2: 128.

24. [James T. Austin,] *Remarks on Dr. Channing's "Slavery," by a Citizen of Massachusetts* (Boston, 1835).

25. Frank Otto Gatell, *John Gorham Palfrey and the New England Conscience* (Cambridge, Mass.: Harvard University Press, 1963), pp. 119-120.

26. Henry Steele Commager, *Theodore Parker* (Boston: Little, Brown, 1936), p. 80.

27. Much has been written about individual Transcendentalists, but surprisingly little about them collectively. The only attempt at a comprehensive account of the whole movement remains Octavius B. Frothingham's *Transcendentalism in New England* (New York, 1876; reprinted with an introduction by Sydney Ahlstrom, Harper Torchbooks, 1959).

28. Ralph Waldo Emerson, "Historic Notes of Life and Letters in New England" (1880), *Complete Works* (Boston, 1911), 10: 325-26.

29. Christopher Pearse Cranch, "Correspondences" (1840), *Poems* (Philadelphia, 1844), p. 41.

30. Ralph Waldo Emerson, undated remark quoted in his *Complete Works*, 10: 552.

31. William Ellery Channing, "Likeness to God" (1828), *Works*, 3: 229; Ralph Waldo Emerson, "Nature" (1836), *Complete Works*, 1: 10.

32. Perry Miller, "From Edwards to Emerson" (1940), reprinted in *Errand into the Wilderness* (Cambridge, Mass.: Harvard University Press, 1956), pp. 184-203. This insight was anticipated by earlier commentators, however; cf. Octavius B. Frothingham's observation: "An instructive chapter . . . might be written, showing that Transcendentalism was a legitimate product of Puritanism." *Boston Unitarianism, 1820-1850* (New York, 1890), p. 26.

33. William R. Hutchison, *The Transcendentalist Ministers: Church Reform in the New England Renaissance* (New Haven: Yale University Press, 1959).

34. Ralph Waldo Emerson, "The Lord's Supper" (1832), *Complete Works*, 11: 19.

35. See Conrad Wright, "Emerson, Barzillai Frost, and the Divinity School Address" (1956), *Liberal Christians*, pp. 41-61.

36. Ralph Waldo Emerson, "An Address Delivered Before the Senior Class in Divinity College, Cambridge" (1838), *Complete Works*, 1: 132.

37. *Ibid.*, pp. 127, 144, 145.

38. Henry Ware, Jr., "The Personality of the Deity" (1838), *Works*, 3: 26-39.

39. John Ware, *Memoir of Henry Ware, Jr.* (Boston, 1846), 2: 188.

40. They were then collected and republished: Francis Bowen, *Critical Essays on a Few Subjects Connected with the History and Present Condition of Speculative Philosophy* (Boston, 1842).

41. Orestes Brownson, "Review of Andrews Norton, *Evidences of the Genuineness of the Four Gospels*, vol. I," *Boston Quarterly Review*, 2 (1839): 88.

42. Andrews Norton, *A Discourse on the Latest Form of Infidelity* (Cambridge, Mass., 1839), p. 11.

43. *Ibid.*, p. 52. (This passage seems to have been added when the address was published.)

44. *Ibid.*, p. 53.

45. [George Ripley,] *"The Latest Form of Infidelity" Examined: A Letter to Mr. Andrews Norton* (Boston, 1839).

46. Octavius B. Frothingham, *George Ripley* (Boston, 1882), p. 37.
47. Andrews Norton to John Gorham Palfrey, April 22, 1840, Andrews Norton Papers, Houghton Library, Harvard University.
48. Selections from the key documents of the debate over miracles are conveniently available in Perry Miller, ed., *The Transcendentalists: An Anthology* (Cambridge, Mass.: Harvard University Press, 1950), pp. 157-246; for an account of the debate, see Hutchison, *The Transcendentalist Ministers*, pp. 52-97.
49. E.g., Levi Blodgett [pseud. for Theodore Parker], *The Previous Question Between Mr. Andrews Norton and His Alumni Moved and Handled* (Boston, 1840).
50. E.g., Andrews Norton, *The Latest Form of Infidelity*, pp. 54-64.
51. John Weiss, *The Life and Correspondence of Theodore Parker* (Boston, 1864), 1: 108-109.
52. As did Andrews Norton in a passage from *Evidences of the Genuineness of the Gospels* (Boston, 1844), vol. II, reprinted as *The Pentateuch and its Relation to the Jewish and Christian Dispensations* (London, 1863).
53. Theodore Parker, "The Transient and Permanent in Christianity" (1841) has been reprinted in *Three Prophets of Religious Liberalism: Channing—Emerson—Parker*, ed. Conrad Wright (Boston: Beacon Press, 1961). See pp. 119-120.
54. *Ibid.*, p. 133.
55. *Ibid.*, p. 139.
56. Christopher R. Eliot, "The Origin and History of the Boston Association of Ministers," MS in Andover-Harvard Theological Library, gives the fullest account.
57. Theodore Parker, "The Hollis Street Council," *The Dial*, 3 (1841): 201-221.
58. Theodore Parker, "The Relation of Jesus to His Age and the Ages" (1844), *Speeches, Addresses, and Occasional Sermons* (Boston, 1860), 1: 21.
59. Arthur B. Ellis, *History of the First Church in Boston* (Boston, 1881), p. 300.
60. Theodore Parker, *A Letter to the Boston Association of Ministers* (1845); quoted in Clarence H. Faust, "The Background of Unitarian Opposition to Transcendentalism," *Modern Philology*, 25 (1938): 319.
61. Quoted in Gannett, *Ezra Stiles Gannett*, p. 229.
62. American Unitarian Association, *Twenty-Eighth Report* (Boston, 1853), esp. p. 21.
63. Arthur Bolster, *James Freeman Clarke* (Boston: Beacon Press, 1954), p. 223. William R. Hutchison concludes that after 1845 the Unitarian majority "seemed pretty well settled in the conviction that Parker was neither a Unitarian nor a Christian." *The Transcendentalist Ministers*, p. 124.
64. See Amos Bronson Alcott, *Record of Conversations on the Gospels, Held in Mr. Alcott's School, Unfolding the Doctrine and Discipline of Human Culture*, two volumes (Boston, 1836-37).
65. See Lindsay Swift, *Brook Farm* (New York, 1900).
66. Arthur M. Schlesinger, Jr., has written *Orestes Brownson: A Pilgrim's Progress* (Boston: Little, Brown, 1939).
67. Perry Miller edited *Margaret Fuller: American Romantic. A Selection From Her Writings and Correspondence* (Ithaca: Cornell University Press, 1963).

68. Thomas Wentworth Higginson, *Massachusetts in Mourning* (Boston, 1854), quoted in Tilden G. Edelstein, *Strange Enthusiasm: A Life of Thomas Wentworth Higginson* (New Haven: Yale University Press, 1968), p. 163.
69. A fine assessment of Hedge is given in George Huntston Williams, *Rethinking the Unitarian Relationship with Protestantism: An Examination of the Thought of Frederic Henry Hedge* (Boston: Beacon Press, 1949).
70. James Freeman Clarke, *Autobiography, Diary, and Correspondence*, ed. Edward Everett Hale (Boston, 1891), is fuller on the early than on the later years of his life. Clarke's course of lectures entitled *Self-Culture: Physical, Intellectual, Moral, and Spiritual* (Boston, 1880 and many subsequent editions) is one of the most revealing examples of nineteenth-century Unitarian thought.
71. See Walter Donald Kring, *Liberals among the Orthodox: Unitarian Beginnings in New York City* (Boston: Beacon Press, 1974).
72. On Gilman, see Daniel Walker Howe, "A Massachusetts Yankee in Senator Calhoun's Court: Samuel Gilman in South Carolina," *New England Quarterly*, 44 (1971): 197-220; also the addresses by Howe and Conrad Wright in *Proceedings of the Unitarian Historical Society*, vol. 17, part 2 (1974). There is an interesting characterization of King in Kevin Starr, *Americans and the California Dream* (New York: Oxford University Press, 1973), pp. 97-105.
73. Quoted in Charles Wendte, *Thomas Starr King* (Boston: Beacon Press, 1921), p. 18.
74. Bolster, *James Freeman Clarke*, p. 267.
75. Henry W. Bellows, *The Suspense of Faith: An Address to the Alumni of the Divinity School* (New York, 1859), p. 37.
76. James Walker, "Difficulties in Parishes," *Christian Examiner*, 9 (1830): 18.

CHAPTER THREE NOTES

1. Henry W. Bellows, *The Suspense of Faith* (New York, 1859).
2. Henry W. Bellows, *The Reformed Church of Christendom, or the Duties of Liberal Churches to the National Faith at this Crisis of Opinion* (Boston, 1865), p. 20.
3. *Monthly Journal* of the A.U.A., 6 (1865): 1-20.
4. For a detailed account of the New York convention, see Conrad Wright, *The Liberal Christians* (Boston: Beacon Press, c. 1970), pp. 81-109.
5. Bellows to R. N. Bellows, April 12, 1865. Bellows Papers, Massachusetts Historical Society (M.H.S.).
6. Edward Everett Hale, "The National Conference of Unitarian Churches," *Christian Examiner* 78 (1865): 427.
7. Francis Ellingwood Abbot, "The Two Confederacies," *Christian Register*, June 24, 1865.
8. Octavius Brooks Frothingham, "The Unitarian Convention and the Times," *Friend of Progress*, 1 (1864-65): 225-230; afterwards reprinted as a tract.
9. *Report of the Convention of Unitarian Churches Held in New York, on the 5th and 6th of April, 1865* (Boston, 1866), pp. 47, 49.

10. *Report of the Second Meeting of the National Conference of Unitarian and Other Christian Churches, Held in Syracuse, N.Y., October 10-11, 1866* (Boston, 1866), p. 10.
11. A number of the conferences founded at this time lasted until the Unitarian-Universalist merger in 1961, when they were superseded by district organizations.
12. This situation lasted until 1925, when the National Conference was merged into the A.U.A. At that time, voting rights were denied to individual members, except for those already enrolled as life members. The list of voting life members becomes smaller and smaller as time passes, but as of the current anniversary year (1975), more than two score names remain. It might be said that the structural reorganization begun by Bellows in 1865, which had as its goal to make denominational organizations directly responsible to the churches, is not even now quite complete.
13. See the Treasurer's Statements in the *Monthly Journal*, 4 (1863): 288; 5 (1864): 290; 7 (1866): 302; 8 (1876): 246.
14. "Report of Samuel A. Eliot," *American Unitarian Association: Annual Report 1900* [Boston, 1900], pp. 8-9.
15. Joseph Henry Allen, *Our Liberal Movement in Theology* (Boston, 1882), pp. 114-115.
16. *Ibid.*, p. 204.
17. John White Chadwick, *Henry W. Bellows: His Life and Character: A Sermon* (New York, 1882), p. 19.
18. Cyrus A. Bartol, "Henry Whitney Bellows," *Unitarian Review*, 17 (1882): 238.
19. Bellows to R. N. Bellows, March 1, 1865.   M.H.S.
20. Douglas C. Stange, "The Conversion of Frederic Dan Huntington (1859): A Failure of Liberalism?" *Historical Magazine of the Protestant Episcopal Church*, 37 (1968): 287-298.
21. Bellows to R. N. Bellows, March 1, 1865.   M.H.S.
22. See Conrad Wright, *The Liberal Christians*, esp. Chapter 1.
23. Bellows to R. N. Bellows, March 1, 1865.   M.H.S.
24. *Report of the Convention*, p. 35.
25. *Christian Register*, April 15, 1865.
26. Bellows to R. N. Bellows, March 1, 1865.   M.H.S.
27. Bellows to J. F. Clarke, March 27, 1865.   M.H.S.
28. John Edward Dirks, *The Critical Theology of Theodore Parker* (New York: Columbia University Press, 1948); H. Shelton Smith, "Was Theodore Parker a Transcendentalist?" *New England Quarterly*, 23 (1950): 351-364.
29. Bellows to R. N. Bellows, March 1, 1865.   M.H.S.
30. Sydney E. Ahlstrom, "Francis Ellingwood Abbot," unpublished dissertation, Harvard, 1951, esp. Chap. 14; Stow Persons, *Free Religion* (New Haven: Yale University Press, c. 1947). Abbot's attack on intuitionalism was originally a lecture given under the auspices of the F.R.A., and entitled "Intuitionalism versus Science, or The Civil War in Free Religion." It was printed as "The Intuitional and Scientific Schools of Free Religion," *The Index*, 2 (1871): 115.
31. Ahlstrom, *op. cit.*, Chap. 12; see also *Opinions of the Justices of the Supreme Judicial Court of New Hampshire in Hale v. Everett, (The Unitarian Church Case)*. For a statement of Abbot's rejection of Christianity, see "The Genius of Christianity and Free Religion," reprinted in Joseph

L. Blau, ed., *American Philosophical Addresses* (New York: Columbia University Press, 1946), pp. 680-708.

32. What was the relative strength of the four groups Bellows discerned in the Unitarian body of 1865? One can at most hazard a guess. In numbers, the Evangelicals and the Radicals were both relatively few; but the radical wing was of more consequence because it was aggressive, while the Evangelicals were passive. Probably the overwhelming majority of Unitarians were Christian Theists, after the style of the Old Rationalists, but open to persuasion. The Broad Church position was doubtless widely held, but latent, needing leadership to bring it to coherence and effectiveness. Bellows and his colleagues supplied this leadership, and succeeded in moving the conservative majority in the direction of a larger inclusiveness. One may well speculate as to what the outcome would have been without Bellows, Hale, and Clarke, to perform this function.

33. F. H. Hedge, *Address Delivered Before the Graduating Class* (Cambridge, 1849), cited in G. H. Williams, *Rethinking the Unitarian Relationship with Protestantism* (Boston: Beacon Press, 1949), p. 33.

34. Henry W. Bellows, *Restatements of Christian Doctrine* (New York, 1860), p. 69; Bellows, *Twenty-Four Sermons* (New York, 1886), p. 383.

35. James Freeman Clarke, *Ten Great Religions* (Boston, 1871), p. 31.

36. Allen, *Our Liberal Movement*, p. 30.

37. Bellows, *Suspense of Faith*, pp. 45, 40.

38. F. H. Hedge, "The Destinies of Ecclesiastical Religion," *Christian Examiner*, 82 (1866): 13, 14.

39. J. F. Clarke, "Union of Churches," *Monthly Journal*, 5 (1864): 201; *Report of the Convention* (1865), p. 21.

40. H. W. Bellows, *A Sequel to "The Suspense of Faith"* (New York, 1859), pp 42, 44-45.

41. Hedge, "Destinies of Ecclesiastical Religion," *op. cit.*, p. 12.

42. Hedge to Bellows, May 3, 1856, reprinted in Ronald V. Wells, *Three Christian Transcendentalists* (New York: Columbia University Press, 1943), p. 214.

43. *Report of the Convention* (1865), p. 39.

44. F. E. Abbot, "The Two Confederacies," *Christian Register*, June 24, 1865.

45. For the events of the Conference, see the *Christian Inquirer*, October 18, 1866; the *Christian Register*, October 13, 20, 1866; and *Report of the Second Meeting* (1866). Abbot's immediate reaction to the meeting may be found in a letter to W. J. Potter, November 21, 1866, quoted at length in Ahlstrom, *op. cit.*, Vol. 2, p. 75; also F. E. Abbot, "The National Unitarian Conference," *Christian Register*, November 17, 1866. Retrospective versions may be found in: F. E. Abbot, "The Battle of Ideas at Syracuse," *The Index*, 6 (1875): 230-231, later reprinted as a tract; F. E. Abbot, "The Royalty of Jesus," *Christian Register*, February 5, 1885; J. F. Clarke, "Mr. Abbot on the Royalty of Jesus," *Christian Register*, February 19, 1885; F. E. Abbot, "Open Letter to Dr. Clarke," *Christian Register*, March 12, 1885; F. E. Abbot, "A Last Word on 'Points of View,'" *Christian Register*, April 9, 1885.

46. Frederic H. Hedge, "The Historic Atonement," Convention Sermon, *Christian Inquirer*, October 18, 1866.

47. F. E. Abbot, "Organization," *The Radical*, 2 (1886): 223.

48. W. J. Potter, *The Free Religious Association: Its Twenty-Five Years and Their Meaning* (Boston, 1892), p. 12.

49. Sydney E. Ahlstrom, "Francis Ellingwood Abbot and the Free Religious Association," *Proceedings of the Unitarian Historical Society*, Vol. 17, Part 2 (1973-74); Stow Persons, *Free Religion*.

50. *Report of the Third Meeting of the National Conference* (Boston, 1868), p. 87.

51. *Report of the Fourth Meeting of the National Conference* (Boston, 1870), p. 123.

52. *Official Report of the Proceedings of the Tenth Meeting of the National Conference* (New York, 1882), p. 26.

53. *Forty-Fifth Anniversary of the American Unitarian Association* (Boston, 1870), p. 23.

54. *Ibid.*, p. 33.

55. John White Chadwick, "The Organization of Our Liberty," *Christian Register*, July 19, 1900. It should be noted that in the spring of 1870 a good deal of tension existed between conservatives and radicals in the denomination, and the Broad Church group was concerned to maintain a balance between them. In February, Dr. James W. Thompson of Jamaica Plain published an article entitled "The Situation" in the *Monthly Review and Religious Magazine* [43: (1870): 117-133] criticizing the spread of free thinking in the denomination, and Edmund H. Sears followed this article with one in the April issue, entitled "The Unitarian Crisis," [43 (1870): 313-328]. To Radicals, and even to many Broad Churchmen, these essays seemed reactionary. See T.B. Forbush to E. E. Hale, February 13, 23, 1870; March 1, 1870; Charles Lowe to Hale, March 5, 1870; Forbush to Hale, February 25, 1871; all in the Hale Papers, Harvard Divinity School. Charles Lowe, then secretary of the A.U.A., addressed the meeting of the Association on May 24, attempting to undercut the right wing move for a creedal or quasi-creedal statement and was sharply criticized as a result. Hepworth's side of the story is told, partly in the words of A. P. Putnam, in Susan Hayes Ward, *George H. Hepworth* (New York, 1903). Hepworth left the Unitarians for the Congregationalists soon afterwards. See Hepworth to Hale, December 28, 1871, H.D.S.

56. Fox to Potter, November 28, 1873, printed in the *Christian Register*, December 13, 1873.

57. Potter to Fox, December 1, 1873, printed in the *Christian Register*, December 13, 1873. The original letter is in A.U.A. Letter Books, Harvard Divinity School.

58. Martha Perry Lowe, *Memoir of Charles Lowe* (Boston, 1884), p. 579.

59. *Christian Register*, September 26, 1874.

60. Since this motion was essentially a gesture of fellowship, Potter construed the vote to be a denial of fellowship; see William J. Potter, *Some Aspects of Unitarianism in Its Past and Present History* (New Bedford, 1874). For the wording of Bellows's motion, see *Report of the Sixth Meeting of the National Conference* (Salem, 1874), p. 241. Potter himself had not attended meetings of the Conference since 1866; lay delegates from New Bedford had not been present since 1870.

61. *Unity*, 15 (1885): 123, 124.

62. J. T. Sunderland, *The Issue in the West* (n.p.), p. 1.

63. The conservatives' account of the Conference is in *The Unitarian*, 1 (1886): 167-169; Gannett's version is in *Unity*, 17 (1886): 161-164.

64. The word "bleach" comes from the Reverend John Snyder of St. Louis, in *The Unitarian*, 1 (1886): 219.

65. Crooker to Grindall Reynolds, June 25, 1886. A.U.A. Letter Books, H.D.S.
66. Forbush to Reynolds, July 13, 1886. A.U.A. Letter Books, H.D.S.
67. W. C. Gannett, "Our Twin Unitarian Superstitions, and How to Get Rid of Them," *Unity*, 17 (1886): 359.
68. *Ibid.*
69. *Unity*, 29 (1892): 105.
70. The satisfaction of conservatives with the outcome may be seen in "Union in the West," *The Unitarian*, 7 (1892): 280-282. The disappointment of Gannett and Jones may be found in W. C. Gannett, "A Dimmed Ideal," *Unity*, 29 (1892): 129-130; and J. Ll. Jones, "Inclusive Religion," *Unity*, 29 (1892): 140-142. But Gannett and Jones had lost support among close associates: Celia P. Woolley, assistant editor of *Unity*, spoke for the resolution in the meeting and defended her vote afterwards; see C. P. Woolley, "The Supplementary Resolution," *Unity*, 29 (1892): 146. The impatience of Fenn, Crothers, and other younger men with the domination of Western Unitarianism by "boss Jones" is bluntly stated in Fenn's unpublished autobiography, used by courtesy of the Reverend Dan Huntington Fenn.
71. The committee proposal was printed in the *Christian Register*, March 29, 1894, p. 194. Of later comments printed in the *Register*, see especially a demurrer by John Cuckson, April 5, 1894, p. 211; the report of a public meeting held in Boston, June 14, 1894, pp. 377-378; and a defence by Charles G. Ames, a member of the committee, September 13, 1894, p. 580. The final text is cited from: *Official Report of the Proceedings of the Fifteenth Meeting of the National Conference* (Boston, 1894), p. 8. Comments on the proposal also appeared in *The Unitarian* and *Unity*.
72. S. J. Barrows, "How the Banner Was Unfurled," *Christian Register*, October 4, 1894, p. 626; "Our National Conference," *The Unitarian*, 9 (1894): 459.
73. Forbush to G. W. Fox, October 5, 1894, A.U.A. Letter Books, H.D.S.; S. J, Barrows, *Christian Register*, October 4, 1894, p. 626. The only sour note came from Jenkin Lloyd Jones, who had not been present at the Conference. It was, he declared, a "temporary settlement"; the Unitarians have once again decided not to dispute, but he predicted that they would not long be satisfied with the result. As for himself, "this revised word is not our banner." At this time, Jones had largely withdrawn from the Western Conference, following the revolt of the younger men, and was much involved in promoting a new organization, the American Congress of Liberal Religious Societies, of which he was the secretary and leading spirit. See "A Temporary Settlement," *Unity*, 33 (1894): 450-451.
74. Emily A. Fifield and Mary Fifield King, *History of the Alliance* (n.p., 1915).
75. The original 25 Beacon Street was located on the other side of the State House from the present building, on the corner of Bowdoin Street.

CHAPTER FOUR NOTES

1. Arthur Cushman McGiffert, Jr., *Samuel Atkins Eliot, 1862-1950* (Claremont, Cal.: privately printed, 1974), p. 1:1.
2. *Ibid.*, p. 2:6.

3. Samuel K. Lothrop, *An Address Delivered at the Opening of the Rooms of the American Unitarian Association, 21 Bromfield Street* (Boston, 1854), p. 13.
4. A.U.A., Board of Directors Minutes, December 14, 1897.
5. McGiffert, *Eliot,* chap. 4.
6. *Ibid.,* chap. 5.
7. *Ibid.,* pp. 6:2, 3.
8. *Ibid.,* p. 5:40.
9. *Ibid.,* p. 3:25.
10. Board of Directors Minutes, February 8, 1898.
11. *Christian Register,* May 24, 1900, p. 566.
12. *Christian Register,* June 1, 1899, p. 613.
13. *Christian Register,* February 22, 1900, p. 220.
14. *Christian Register,* February 15, 1900, p. 175.
15. *Christian Register,* April 26, 1900, p. 450.
16. McGiffert, *Eliot,* p. 6:11.
17. *Christian Register,* January 11, 1900, p. 50.
18. *Christian Register,* February 8, 1900, p. 141.
19. Board of Directors Minutes, June 12, 1900.
20. A.U.A. Scrapbook, 1892-1914. U.U.A. Archives.
21. Samuel A. Eliot, circular letter, October 15, 1907. A.U.A. Scrapbook, 1892-1914.
22. *Christian Register,* January 4, 1900, p. 24.
23. Board of Directors Minutes, March 10, 1903.
24. McGiffert, *Eliot,* p. 11:24.
25. *Preliminary Account and Program of the First Congress of the National Federation of Religious Liberals,* April 27-30, 1909. A.U.A. Scrapbook, 1892-1914.
26. Board of Directors Minutes, December 8, 1914.
27. *Ibid.,* November 10, 1914.
28. *Ibid.,* March 14, 1911.
29. McGiffert, *Eliot,* pp. 6:42, 43.
30. Board of Directors Minutes, October 14, 1913.
31. Board of Directors Minutes, February 10, 1920; McGiffert, *Eliot,* chap. 16.
32. Clara Cook Helvie, "Unitarian Woman Ministers," unpublished typescript, 1928, p. 100. U.U.A. Archives.
33. *Christian Register,* September 3, 1914, p. 860.
34. *Christian Register,* August 6, 1914, p. 748.
35. *Christian Register,* August 20, 1914, p. 793.
36. *Christian Register,* September 3, 1914, p. 841.
37. *Christian Register,* September 10, 1914, p. 883.
38. *Christian Register,* October 15, 22, 1914, pp. 1002-1003, 1022-1023.
39. *Christian Register,* December 10, 1914, pp. 1188-1189.
40. *Christian Register,* December 24, 1914, p. 1246.
41. *Christian Register,* December 31, 1914, pp. 1255-1256.
42. *Christian Register,* May 17, 1917, p. 460.
43. McGiffert, *Eliot,* p. 13:19.
44. Board of Directors Minutes, November 13, 1917.
45. *Christian Register,* May 17, 1917, p. 479.
46. *Official Report of the Proceedings of the Twenty-Seventh Meeting of the General Conference of Unitarian and Other Christian Churches,* Montreal, September 25-28, 1917 (Boston, Geo. H. Ellis, 1918), p. 49.

47. *Ibid.,* p. 51.
48. *Ibid.,* pp. 53-58.
49. *Ibid.,* p. 62.
50. *Ibid.,* pp. 60, 64.
51. *Ibid.,* p. 3.
52. *Ibid.,* pp. 9-10.
53. *Ibid.,* p. 12.
54. *Ibid.,* p. 14.
55. Board of Directors Minutes, April 9, 1918.
56. John Haynes Holmes, *I Speak for Myself* (New York: Harper & Brothers, 1959), chap. 16.
57. McGiffert, *Eliot,* pp. 13:21, 13:1.
58. Louis C. Cornish, ed., *Transylvania in 1922* (Boston: Beacon Press, 1923), p. 1. This section is based on the author's article, "Liberals and Liberalism Since 1900," *Proceedings of the Unitarian Historical Society,* Vol. 15, Part 1 (1964), pp. 1-25.
59. Cornish, *Transylvania in 1922,* chap. 1.
60. Louis C. Cornish, *Work and Dreams and the Wide Horizon* (Boston: Beacon Press, 1937), p. 312.
61. Frances E. F. Cornish, *Louis Craig Cornish, Interpreter of Life* (Boston: Beacon Press, c. 1953), pp. 55-57.
62. For Capek see Samuel A. Eliot, ed., *The Pilots.* Heralds of a Liberal Faith, vol. 4. (Boston: Beacon Press, c. 1952), pp. 72-75. On the historical and cultural context of Czechoslovakia's emergence to national consciousness, see Tomas G. Masaryk, *The Meaning of Czech History,* ed. Rene Wellek (Chapel Hill: Univ. of North Carolina Press, 1974).
63. Cornish, *Cornish,* p. 80.
64. *Ibid.,* p. 83.
65. *Ibid.,* p. 85. See also Cornish, *Work and Dreams,* pp. 355-397 and Louis C. Cornish, *The Philippines Calling* (Philadelphia: Dorrance and Co., c. 1942). Another perspective is that of Norman S. Binsted, "The Philippine Independent Church," *Historical Magazine of the Protestant Episcopal Church,* 27 (1958): 209-246.
66. Board of Directors Minutes, April 14, 1925.
67. *Ibid.,* May 13, 1919.
68. McGiffert, *Eliot,* p. 7:26.
69. Board of Directors Minutes, March 11, 1924.
70. *Ibid.,* May 22, 1924.
71. McGiffert, *Eliot,* p. 18:6.
72. Board of Directors Minutes, April 26, 1927.
73. *Ibid.,* April 11, 1922.
74. *Christian Register,* October 13, 1927, p. 810.
75. George H. Williams, ed., *The Harvard Divinity School* (Boston, Beacon Press, c. 1954), pp. 186-210.
76. "It is needless for me to point out . . . [said President Franklin C. Southworth in June, 1925] how utterly and absurdly inadequate has proved the old-time seminary to educate religious leaders for the new world. Surely it must now be apparent to all who are capable of observing the tendencies of their time that ministers of religion should be trained for their task, not in isolation from those human contacts which constitute the distinctive features of modern life, but in those centers of population where competition is fiercest, where the class struggle is most desperate,

where conditions exist which pull men down, and where agencies also exist, or at least may be created, to lift men up. It goes without saying that Chicago is such a city." *Meadville Theological School Quarterly Bulletin*, Vol. 22, No. 3 (April, 1928), p. 18.

77. McGiffert, *Eliot*, p. 11:35.
78. Board of Directors Minutes, April 12, 1904.
79. McGiffert, *Eliot*, p. 11:37.
80. Earl M. Wilbur, "How the History Came to be Written," *Proceedings of the Unitarian Historical Society*, Vol. 9, Part 1 (1951), pp. 5-23.
81. McGiffert, *Eliot*, p. 10:24.
82. "The Work of the American Unitarian Association," (1903), anonymous pamphlet in A.U.A. Scrapbook, 1892-1914.
83. *Christian Register*, December 15, 1927, p. 1002.
84. John Haynes Holmes, *The Revolutionary Function of the Modern Church* (New York: G. P. Putnam's Sons, 1912), p. 175.
85. "A Service for Fellowship Day," in A.U.A. Scrapbook, 1892-1914.
86. Eliot, *The Pilots*, pp. 235-236. See also Max F. Daskam and others, "William Laurence Sullivan as We Knew Him," in Max F. Daskam, ed., *The Flaming Spirit* (New York: Abingdon Press, 1961), pp. 16-21.
87. James Hastings Nichols, *History of Christianity 1650-1950* (New York: Ronald Press, c. 1956), pp. 302-304.
88. William L. Sullivan, *Under Orders* (New York: Richard R. Smith, 1944), p. 158.
89. A Modernist [William L. Sullivan], *Letters to His Holiness Pope Pius X* (Chicago: Open Court Publishing Co., 1914), pp. 31, 86, 188.
90. Charles Francis Potter, *The Preacher and I* (New York: Crown Publishers, 1951), p. 376.
91. Carleton Winston, *This Circle of Earth* (New York: G. P. Putnam's Sons, 1942), pp. 66-82.
92. Potter, *Preacher and I*, p. 98.
93. Charles H. Lyttle, *Freedom Moves West* (Boston: Beacon Press, c. 1952), p. 242.
94. *Ibid.*, chap. 11. See also David B. Parke, ed., *The Epic of Unitarianism* (Boston: Starr King Press, c. 1957), pp. 122-131.
95. Raymond B. Bragg, "An Historical Note," *The Humanist*, 13 (1953): 62-63.
96. "The Humanist Manifesto: Twenty Years After," *The Humanist*, 13 (1953): 58-61.
97. *Christian Register*, September 14, 1933, p. 604.
98. McGiffert, *Eliot*, p. 8:1.
99. *Christian Register*, May 30, 1912, p. 527. See also McGiffert, *Eliot*, p. 7:25.
100. *Christian Register*, May 19, 1927, p. 400.
101. *Christian Register*, October 27, 1927, p. 841.
102. Board of Directors Minutes, May 9, 1927.
103. McGiffert, *Eliot*, p. 7:17.
104. *Ibid.*, p. 10:36.
105. *Christian Register*, July 7, 1927, p. 554.
106. Board of Directors Minutes, June 29, 1927.
107. *Christian Register*, July 7, 1927, p. 550.
108. *Christian Register*, October 20, 1927, p. 821.
109. *Christian Register*, October 27, 1927, p. 841.
110. Board of Directors Minutes, February 14, 1928.
111. *Ibid.*, November 8, 1927.

112. *Ibid.*, February 14, 1928.
113. *Christian Register,* October 20, 1927, p. 834.
114. Board of Directors Minutes, April 11, 1932.
115. *Ibid.*, November 23, 1931.
116. *Ibid.*, November 10, 1931.
117. L. C. Cornish, circular letter to the churches, February 2, 1934.
118. *Christian Register,* February 16, 1933, p. 103.
119. Board of Directors Minutes, December 11, 1928.
120. *Ibid.*, May 14, 1929, January 13, 1931.
121. Ethelred Brown, "A Brief History of the Harlem Unitarian Church," mimeograph, September, 1949. U.U.A. Archives.
122. *Christian Register,* February 8, 1934, p. 97.
123. David B. Parke, "The Historical and Religious Antecedents of the New Beacon Series in Religious Education (1937)." Ph.D. dissertation (unpublished), Boston University, 1965, p. 180.
124. Board of Directors Minutes, February 14, 1933.
125. *Ibid.*, October 10, 1933.
126. *Ibid.*, March 13, 1928, April 10, 1928, February 11, 1930, March 11, 1930, November 18, 1930.
127. A full discussion of the origins and development of the New Beacon Series under Mrs. Fahs's leadership is found in the author's dissertation cited above. A briefer account is found in his essay, "Liberals and Liberalism Since 1900," *op. cit.,* pp. 15-20.
128. Board of Directors Minutes, October 9, 1934.
129. *Christian Register,* April 26, 1934, p. 282.
130. Lewis G. Wilson, Secretary, Committee on Comity and Fellowship, in circular letter, A.U.A. Scrapbook, 1892-1914.
131. McGiffert, *Eliot,* pp. 14:13, 14.
132. Letter to the *Christian Leader,* July 23, 1927, reprinted in the *Christian Register,* July 28, 1927, p. 609.
133. *Christian Register,* January 12, 1933, p. 20.
134. *Christian Register,* November 10, 1927, p. 886.
135. *Christian Register,* January 12, 1933, p. 22.
136. *Christian Register,* October 26, 1933, p. 695.
137. Letter to the *Christian Register,* January 10, 1935, p. 28.
138. *Christian Register,* February 7, 1935, p. 96.
139. Board of Directors Minutes, October 31, 1935.
140. *Christian Register,* June 16, 1927, p. 493.
141. Board of Directors Minutes, May 28, 1909.
142. *Ibid.*, January 14, 1930.
143. *Ibid.*, April 14, 1931.
144. *Ibid.*, December 3, 1930.
145. *Christian Register,* February 7, 1935. See also Board of Directors Minutes, April 9, 1935.
146. Board of Directors Minutes, February 13, 1935.
147. *Ibid.*, March 12, 1929.
148. *Ibid.*, April 11, 1932.
149. *Ibid.*, April 26, 1934. See also December 12, 1933 and April 10, 1934.
150. *Christian Register,* May 17, 1934, p. 381.
151. Letter to the *Christian Register,* January 18, 1934, p. 44.
152. Board of Directors Minutes, October 10, 1933.

CHAPTER FIVE NOTES

1. American Unitarian Association, *Annual Report* (1933-34), p. 11.
2. Interview, Dr. James Luther Adams, July 8, 1968.
3. A.U.A., *Annual Report* (1933-34), pp. 60-61.
4. Published by the Institute of Social and Religious Research in collaboration with the Church Federation of St. Louis (New York, 1924).
5. Commission of Appraisal, *Unitarians Face a New Age* (Boston, 1936), p. 310.
6. *Ibid.,* p. 23.
7. Interview, Dr. Leslie T. Pennington, October 19, 1968.
8. For a detailed biography of Eliot, see Carol R. Morris, "Frederick May Eliot, President of the American Unitarian Association (1937-1958)," Ph.D. dissertation (unpublished), Boston University, 1970.
9. Carol R. Morris, "The Election of Frederick May Eliot to the Presidency of A.U.A.," *Proceedings of the Unitarian Historical Society,* Vol. 17, Part 1 (1970-72), p. 3.
10. *Ibid.,* pp. 3-6.
11. *Christian Register,* May 13, 1937, p. 311.
12. This freedom for a broader fellowship and a broader base for theological dialogue has been regarded by some as one of Eliot's greatest contributions. Interview, Rev. William P. Jenkins, June 12, 1968.
13. The Interim Commission of the Commission of Appraisal met after the report was made to the May Meetings, 1936. See "Memorandum Concerning the Work of the Interim Commission on Planning and Review," undated but written in all probability by Eliot after January 14, 1937. Archives of the U.U.A., 25 Beacon Street, Boston.
14. *Ibid.,* p. 1.
15. Frederick May Eliot, "Sign Posts on the Horizon," *Christian Register,* November 11, 1937, p. 663.
16. *Ibid.,* p. 664.
17. *Ibid.*
18. *Ibid.,* p. 665.
19. A.U.A., *Annual Report* (1934-35), p. 57.
20. For the contribution of Mrs. Fahs, see Edith F. Hunter, *Sophia Lyon Fahs* (Boston: Beacon Press, 1966). This sensitive and brilliant biography is essential for an understanding of developments in religious education in this period.
21. David B. Parke, "The Historical and Religious Antecedents of the New Beacon Series in Religious Education," p. 381. Ph.D. dissertation (unpublished), Boston University, 1965. In addition to the works by Hunter and Parke, the following also should be consulted: Robert L'H. Miller, "The Educational Philosophy of the New Beacon Series in Religious Education." Th.D. dissertation (unpublished), Boston University, 1957.
22. Interview, Dr. Frank O. Holmes, June 12, 1969.
23. James Ford Lewis, "History of the Unitarian Service Committee," p. 12. Ph.D. dissertation (unpublished), University of California, 1952.
24. *Ibid.,* p. 14.
25. *Ibid.,* p. 15.
26. George F. Patterson to Eliot, March 26, 1943. U.U.A. Archives.
27. Eliot to Genevieve Steefel, February 28, 1944. U.U.A. Archives.
28. *Christian Register,* December, 1942, p. 424.

29. A.U.A., "Board Records" (October 19, 1944), pp. 1502-1503.

30. *Christian Register*, July, 1942, pp. 237-260.

31. F. M. Eliot, "A Basic Faith for a United World," *Christian Register*, October, 1944, p. 361.

32. Albert C. Dieffenbach, "The Church of the Larger Fellowship," *Christian Register*, October, 1944, p. 361.

33. "The Faith Behind Freedom," *Christian Register*, June, 1943, pp. 200-201.

34. Stephen H. Fritchman, "Filling the Unitarian Lamps," *Christian Register*, May, 1944, pp. 162-163.

35. A.U.A., "Board Records" (January 10, 1945), p. 1520.

36. F. M. Eliot, "The Future of the *Christian Register*," *Christian Register*, April 1, 1941, p. 124.

37. "Minutes of the Annual Meeting of the American Unitarian Association," 1947, pp. 71-75. The Fritchman controversy is treated in detail in Carol R. Morris, "Frederick May Eliot," pp. 287-322.

38. Personal recollections of the Beacon Press in these years by Edward Darling were published in successive issues of *The Beacon*, beginning Vol. 2, No. 2 (February, 1965).

39. Darling, *op. cit.*, Vol. 2, No. 2 (February, 1965).

40. Darling, *op. cit.*, Vol. 2, No. 3 (March, 1965).

41. *Ibid.*

42. Laile E. Bartlett, *Bright Galaxy: Ten Years of Unitarian Fellowships* (Boston: Beacon Press, c. 1960), p. 36. See also Laile E. Bartlett, "Unitarian Fellowships," in *Take a Giant Step* [1967], pamphlet reprint of addresses at the 1967 U.U.A. General Assembly, and Laile E. Bartlett, "Unitarian Fellowships: a Case Study in Liberal Religious Development." Ph.D. dissertation (unpublished) University of California, Berkeley, 1966.

43. Bartlett, *Bright Galaxy*, pp. 36-40.

44. *Take a Giant Step*, p. 19.

45. Cf. esp. Bartlett, *Bright Galaxy*, Chap. 5.

46. *Christian Register*, Mid-Summer, 1957, p. 26.

47. F. M. Eliot, "Unitarian Horizons," *Christian Register*, June, 1957, p. 7.

48. *Christian Register*, Mid-Summer, 1957, p. 26. Gibbs was for several years Director of the Department of Church Extension.

49. Alfred P. Stiernotte, *Frederick May Eliot: An Anthology* (Boston: Beacon Press, c. 1959, p. xxi.

50. Eileen Layton (Deister) served as the last President of A.U.Y. Clara Mayo, now Professor of Social Psychology at Boston University, served as L.R.Y.'s first President.

51. *Christian Register*, Mid-Summer, 1959, p. 21.

52. The Syracuse meeting was reported in the *Christian Register*, December, 1959, pp. 19-24.

53. Donald S. Harrington, "We Are That Faith!" *Christian Register*, Mid-Summer, 1960, pp. 3-6.

PRESIDENTS OF THE ASSOCIATION

1825—1836	Aaron Bancroft
1837—1844	Ichabod Nichols
1844—1845	Joseph Story
1845—1847	Orville Dewey
1847—1851	Ezra Stiles Gannett
1851—1858	Samuel Kirkland Lothrop
1858—1859	Edward Brooks Hall
1859—1862	Frederick Henry Hedge
1862—1865	Rufus Phineas Stebbins
1865—1867	John Gorham Palfrey
1867—1870	Thomas Dawes Eliot
1870—1872	Henry Chapin
1872—1876	John Wells
1876—1886	Henry Purkitt Kidder
1886—1887	George Dexter Robinson
1887—1895	George Silsbee Hale
1895—1897	John Davis Long
1897—1900	Carroll Davidson Wright
1900—1927	Samuel Atkins Eliot
1927—1937	Louis Craig Cornish
1937—1958	Frederick May Eliot
1958—1961	Dana McLean Greeley

SECRETARIES OF THE ASSOCIATION

1825—1831	Ezra Stiles Gannett
1829—1834	Henry Ware Jr.
1831—1833	Alexander Young
1833—1834	Samuel Barrett
1834—1835	Jason Whitman
1835—1847	Charles Briggs
1847—1848	William Greenleaf Eliot
1848—1850	Frederick West Holland
1850—1853	Calvin Lincoln
1853—1859	Henry Adolphus Miles
1859—1861	James Freeman Clarke
1861—1865	George William Fox
1865—1871	Charles Lowe
1871—1881	Rush Rhees Shippen
1881—1894	Grindall Reynolds
1894—1898	George Batchelor
1898—1900	Samuel Atkins Eliot
1900—1908	Charles Elliot St. John
1908—1915	Lewis Gilbert Wilson
1916—1925	Louis Craig Cornish
1925—1930	Parker Endicott Marean
1930—1937	Walter Reid Hunt
1937—1945	Palfrey Perkins
1945—1953	Dana McLean Greeley
1953—1961	Walter Donald Kring

MODERATORS OF THE ASSOCIATION

1938—Sanford Bates
1940—Mrs. Aurelia Henry Reinhardt
1942—Philip C. Nash
1944—Justice Harold H. Burton
1946—Dr. Winifred Overholser
1948—George D. Stoddard
1950—Ernest Boyd MacNaughton
1952—Dexter Perkins
1954—William Roger Greeley
1956—H. Clay Burkholder
1958—Mrs. Emily Taft Douglas
1960—Dr. James R. Killian Jr.

PRESIDENTS OF THE NATIONAL CONFERENCE OF UNITARIAN AND OTHER CHRISTIAN CHURCHES*

1865—70	Thomas D. Eliot
1871—80	Ebenezer Rockwood Hoar
1881—82	John D. Long
1883—84	Ebenezer Rockwood Hoar
1885—90	Samuel F. Miller
1891	(Office unfilled)
1892	George William Curtis
1893—94	(Office unfilled)
1895—1901	George F. Hoar
1902—08	Carroll D. Wright
1909	(Office unfilled)
1910—11	Horace Davis
1912—14	Charles W. Eliot
1915—1925	William Howard Taft

* after 1911 the name became the General Conference of Unitarian and other Christian Churches.

Index